158.24
H314s

Saying It So He'll Listen

Dr. David Hawkins

Title Withdrawn

Edison Branch Library
18400 Joy Rd.
Detroit, MI 48228
(313) 852-4515

HARVEST HOUSE PUBLISHERS

EUGENE, OREGON

OCT 1 9 2005

ED

Unless otherwise indicated, all Scripture quotations are taken from the HOLY BIBLE, NEW INTERNATIONAL VERSION®. NIV®. Copyright©1973, 1978, 1984 by the International Bible Society. Used by permission of Zondervan. All rights reserved.

Verses marked NASB are taken from the New American Standard Bible®, © 1960, 1962, 1963, 1968, 1971, 1972, 1973, 1975, 1977 by The Lockman Foundation. Used by permission. (www.Lockman.org)

Cover by Koechel Peterson & Associates, Inc., Minneapolis, Minnesota

Cover photo © Tom Henry

This book includes stories in which the author has changed people's names and some details of their situations to protect privacy.

SAYING IT SO HE'LL LISTEN
Copyright © 2005 by David Hawkins
Published by Harvest House Publishers
Eugene, Oregon 97402
www.harvesthousepublishers.com

Hawkins, David, 1951–
  Saying it so he'll listen / David Hawkins.
    p. cm.
  ISBN 0-7369-1504-4 (pbk.)
  1. Interpersonal communication—Religious aspects—Christianity. 2. Interpersonal communication—Sex differences 3. Marriage—Religious aspects—Christianity.
  I. Title.
  BV4597.53.C64H39 2005
  158.2'4—dc22

                                                           2004016662

All rights reserved. No part of this publication may be reproduced, stored in a retrieval system, or transmitted in any form or by any means—electronic, mechanical, digital, photocopy, recording, or any other—except for brief quotations in printed reviews, without the prior permission of the publisher.

Printed in the United States of America

05 06 07 08 09 10 11 12 / VP-CF / 10 9 8 7 6 5 4 3 2 1

This book is dedicated to the countless women who have entrusted their stories to me in the hope that they could learn new skills to effectively communicate with their man.

Acknowledgments

Being a man, I have never experienced pregnancy. However, I believe that completing a book must be something like giving birth. I have labored while creating books and waited anxiously for them to be born.

I have not been alone in the birthing process. At this point in my writing career I have compiled a wonderful support cast who share a vision for my work. I am sure that they have been waiting anxiously too. I want to mention a few of them here.

The largest support cast is the team of incredible professionals at Harvest House Publishers. Their entire staff, too many to mention, encourage and allow me to write what God has placed on my heart. They also run me around the country at a breakneck pace, but I suppose that goes with the territory.

I must give special mention to two guys at Harvest House. Gene Skinner has become my "personal editor." How cool is that? He has been with me for several books now, and for reasons still unclear to me, sticks with me and says he even rather enjoys the process. Thanks, Gene, for making each book stronger and better.

Terry Glaspey is the quiet man behind the scenes who talks the folks in charge at Harvest House into letting me write these books. I'm not sure how you do that, but keep it up. For believing in me, Terry, I am profoundly appreciative. Thank you.

My support cast continues with my parents, Hank and Rose Hawkins. Yes, I've mentioned them before, but they really do encourage me and I love them for that, among other reasons. Thanks, Mom and Dad—and keep selling my books. You know how much I love you.

Perhaps the most critical elements of my support cast are Jim and Christie. They are my personal power crew. You guys read my manuscript, chapter after chapter, nudge me forward, get excited with me, and offer helpful feedback. I appreciate all your editing efforts. I really am trying to learn to take constructive criticism. Thanks Jim and Christie.

Finally, I want to thank the Lord for this chance to write. I never take the opportunity for granted. It is a wonderful, creative outlet for me, and I have some sense of how blessed I am. I encourage everyone to find that special place where they feel able to express themselves. Writing does that for me, and I am grateful for it.

Contents

ONE

Everybody's Talking at Me

*Conflict creates the fire of effects and emotions;
and like every fire it has two aspects:
that of burning and that of giving light.*

CARL JUNG

In the crowded Atlanta airport terminal, two young children bounce up and down, tugging at their parents' arms and begging for ice cream. Their bodies can't contain their excitement about flying and the family vacation. Their parents, however, are struggling with carry-ons, tickets, and directions to their check-in counter. They are preoccupied and annoyed, trying to hold off the children with terse phrases about "spoiling lunch" and "too expensive." The children are gradually reduced to whining, and the parents' angry responses escalate to threats. They raise their voices more than they intend to and notice an older couple inadvertently glancing their way.

The older couple does not intend to eavesdrop and quickly resume their own conversation. The man simultaneously scans his itinerary, squints at the arrival and departure monitor, and checks his watch. Their plane is running late, and he is anxiously muttering to his wife that they might miss a connecting flight in another city. She listens intently, pats his arm, and reassures him that all will be fine. Her calm smile soothes him, and he gratefully squeezes her wrinkled hand, sighs contentedly, and smiles at a younger couple seated nearby.

The younger man is very animated. Is his story really that exciting, or is he just trying to win her attention? The woman appears weary and uninterested as he drones on and on. She doesn't want to be rude, but she tries to end the conversation by focusing her attention on the brooding Atlanta skies. He obviously picks up on her subtle rejection, and his rapid-fire chatter gives way to quiet pouting. He doesn't understand that she simply does not have the energy to engage with him.

In all three little groups, people are talking, but not everyone is listening. In one conversation, the people feel connected to each other. In the others, people feel irritated or neglected. One person is receiving exactly what he needs—assurance and comfort. Others are gaining nothing for their efforts.

Effective Communication

As we see in the airport conversations, the word *communication* applies to a broad range of interactions. *Effective communication* is much more specific. Is one-way communication effective? What about communication that ignores the emotions of the hearers? Or communication that doesn't achieve its intended purpose? My goal in this book is to help you make your communication more effective. Communication experts Susan Heitler and Abigail Hirsch tell us in their book *The Power of Two* that effective communication does not come naturally. "Talking and listening about sensitive issues in a marriage takes special skills to keep the dialogue connection open and the information flowing smoothly and safely."[1]

If we choose not to learn and use these special skills, we will invariably settle for ineffective communication. We may *miscommunicate* by not speaking or listening carefully enough. Miscommunication is a frequent cause of disagreements. We may *communicate thoughtlessly* by ignoring other people's needs. We may *communicate dishonestly* by saying whatever we want to get what we want.

Distorted communication contains exaggerations, extreme dramatizations, and twisted facts. People use *passive-aggressive communication* when they tell you what you want to hear and then talk behind your back or do exactly what they want to do. Somehow, they "forget" to do what they have promised. Outright *aggressive communication* includes plenty of blunt, in-your-face comments but little or no genuine concern. *Indirect communication* beats around the bush without really saying what needs to be said.

I consider myself to be a student of the art of communication because I know it is a critical building block in every healthy relationship. This is not new news. Communication has always been the foundation of every good marriage. Take a look at couples that are doing well, and you will see effective communication. Conversely, if you examine the lives of couples whose relationship is filled with tension and conflict, you will see something quite different. Failure to learn these skills can, tragically, lead to the demise of a marriage.

In this book, we are seeking the clear, convincing communication that carries so much positive potential for relationships. Honest, sensitive, and authentic communication holds the key to getting important messages through to your man. And that wonderful level of communication is available to you.

You Can Get There

We have heard for years that men are from different planets than women and that any meeting of these two minds is virtually impossible. Women communicate from their left brains, we are told, and men from their right brains.

I do not agree with the cynics who tell us that effective communication with men is impossible. I do not think that carrying on a meaningful conversation with your spouse is as unlikely or as chance-driven as winning a mega-million-dollar lottery. If we can land a man on the moon, discover the code to DNA, and find cures for diseases, then we can certainly figure out how men and women can communicate effectively.

Although I am confident that we can find answers, I don't think they are apt to jump out and bite us on the nose. We must work to discover truths that lead to real listening, real sharing, and real communication. We will need to overcome obstacles. But trust me—they are surmountable.

As we begin, I encourage you to tune out the views of those who insist that your man will never take you seriously. He can listen. In fact, he really wants to relate to you, and you can make that happen if you follow the advice contained in this book. I have led others down this healing path and can do the same for you. But first you must believe you can get there. We may feel discouraged at times with how our communication is or is not working, but we find comfort in the words of Martin Luther King, who tirelessly preached that "unarmed truth and unconditional love will have the final word in reality."[2]

Everybody's Responsibility

As we begin our journey together, let's be clear about this point: Communication is the responsibility of everyone involved. Whether we are talking about a group of people, such as those at your church or workplace, or more intimate encounters between a husband and wife, communication involves all parties. Each must come to the table prepared to engage in honest, effective communication.

After nearly 30 years of clinical experience, I know that rarely does everyone arrive at the table prepared to follow healthy rules for effective communication—the listening and speaking tools that I will share in this book. All too often, the table is lopsided. Too often, only one party (usually the woman) comes prepared for an honest encounter. What is one to do?

In a marriage where only one partner is willing to work hard at healthy sharing, strategies are available for engaging the resistor. Before you sink into despair or start feeling sorry for yourself, rest assured that you will be empowered by the tools offered in this book. *Saying It So He'll Listen* offers just what the title promises: ways to say what is most important to you so that he will listen, take you seriously, and embark with you on a journey of change.

Is success guaranteed? Yes and no. Can we change other people? Yes and no.

We cannot directly change another person. What we can do is set about to change ourselves and the way we communicate. When we do so, the other partner is much more likely to change. Remember, a marriage and family are dynamic, living organisms, and each part affects the others. When one part changes, the others must change in the process.

Take heart. You can be an instrument of change. In this book, you will learn how to gain the inside track to your man. These tools will be invaluable as you begin changing old, stale patterns of relating.

Brewing Problems

The alarm beeped loud and long, and the radio began blaring rock music that left Kim and her husband, Steve, groping for the off switch. Sunlight streaked through the curtains of their suburban bedroom. In the kitchen, their coffeemaker automatically began brewing a fresh pot of coffee to prepare them for the workday.

The new day gave Steve and Kim a respite from the struggle that was sapping energy from their 12-year marriage. They considered their relationship strong and were dedicated to one another, but one lingering issue plagued them like a nagging toothache. They dulled their pain by working, staying busy around the house, raising three children, and maintaining an active church life.

Kim and Steve crawled out of bed, offering only a "Good morning" to each other as they began their rituals—preparing their kids for school and then readying themselves for work.

Once the kids were set in motion, they moved to the kitchen to grab a cup of coffee. Kim looked at Steve, wondering if the moment was right to bring up "the topic" again.

"Can we talk when you get home tonight?" Kim asked tentatively.

"About what?" Steve responded as he fumbled with the lid to the creamer.

"Steve," she said with a hint of exasperation. "You know about what. We still have to talk about Karen. She's really upset with you."

"Well, as far as I'm concerned there's not much to talk about. She needs to change her attitude."

Kim felt her body grow tense. Were they going to reach yet another impasse over how Steve was treating her daughter from a former marriage?

"She's upset because of how you treat her, Steve."

"And I treat her that way because of how she treats me and our kids," he said firmly. "You need to recognize that."

After getting ready for work, Steve grabbed his coffee and coat, gave Kim a peck on the cheek, and headed for the door.

"Gotta go. Have a good day. Are you going to call the Johnsons about coming to dinner this Sunday?"

"Yes, I'll take care of it. Have a good day at work."

Kim watched Steve head out the door, feeling annoyed and still unsure of how to resolve this ongoing issue between her husband and daughter. Steve seemed able to put things behind him, but Kim knew that she would remain upset for much of the morning.

The problem had been brewing for the past year. Kim and Steve thought that the families were blending well, but then Karen dove headlong into adolescence. She began to question many of Steve's decisions and methods of discipline. The more she picked at him, the more annoyed he became. Kim seemed able to handle Karen's irritability and tests easier than Steve. But then, she was Karen's biological mother.

This Isn't Working

For the next several months, nothing changed between Kim and Steve. Kim kept trying to talk to him about the tension between him and Karen, but his only response was to blame Karen for the problem. Although Kim loved Steve and wanted to do everything possible to save their marriage, her resentment was growing. After failing to get Steve to engage in an honest discussion of the issue, she asked him to consider counseling. Steve was reluctant, but with some effort, Kim was finally able to convince him that counseling was in his best interest and the best interest of their marriage.

Steve was a large man, 36 years old, with a big belly that hung over his waistband. In spite of his size, he dressed sharply in a bright white dress shirt and tailored blazer. He carried an air of quiet confidence that bordered on smugness. He had a firm, chiseled chin that exaggerated his presence and a quick, sarcastic wit that he used as a weapon when annoyed. He deftly fired shots at Kim whenever he felt threatened. The sales skills he'd developed in the advertising department at the local newspaper were very apparent.

Kim was slender, also 36 years old, with unruly long, blonde hair. She kept brushing it out of her face, grimacing each time she did so. I imagined that she could be quite attractive if not for her sunken cheeks and puffy eyes. I could see how she would be effective in her job as an elementary school principal: She was orderly, eloquent, and forceful. But the wind had left her sails. Her power appeared spent, her effectiveness used up on the problems of too many children, or perhaps too many struggles with her husband.

Steve and Kim loved one another and had no intention of ending their marriage, but the issue regarding Kim's daughter would not go away. It was a raw topic, and each time they bumped into it, it seemed to take something out of them. When they finally reached my office, the issue had been brewing for more than a year. Their marriage had worked relatively well until Kim's daughter, Karen, had rather suddenly, and perhaps hormonally, found a new source of independence. Although she had spent her formative years with her stepfather and had called him Dad, she had suddenly begun referring to him as Steve. Karen now wondered aloud about the need to spend more time with her "real father," who lived in a nearby town.

For Kim, this was a painful reminder of her past marriage. For Steve, the message seemed to be that regardless of how hard he tried, he would never fully be Karen's father. Karen used this vulnerable issue to her advantage when annoyed with her parents. She would compare parenting skills, accusing Steve of being too harsh in his discipline. She also brought back gifts her biological father would give her and flaunt them in front of her half-siblings.

Like many other couples, Steve and Kim kept rehearsing their problem. Kim kept shouting her version of things—that Steve gave preferential treatment to their two boys—and Steve kept offering simple, pointed rebuttals—that he was meting out discipline because of Karen's "spiteful attitude." Kim would complain and try, to no avail, to get Steve to ease up on Karen. Steve would counter by pointing out all the ways Kim was reinforcing their daughter's willful defiance. As they engaged in this struggle, their positions solidified, and they could feel themselves losing ground in their marriage.

Early in our work, I decided to try one of Dr. Phil's tactics:

"Is this approach working for you two?" I said, smiling. "It looks very painful, and I can't imagine that either of you feels good about it."

"You ought to live in our home and deal with it on a daily basis," Kim said.

"What is the 'it'?" I asked.

"The sarcasm. The biting words toward me and Karen. I don't feel like he hears a word I say. I can't have a serious conversation with him."

"Not when you talk to me the way you do," he countered. "You are forever defending Karen. You don't know how it feels to be the 'ugly stepfather.'"

"Hold on for a minute," I said firmly. "Can we agree on at least one thing? Can we agree that what you have been trying so far, whatever we decide that to be, is not working?"

"That's for sure," Kim blurted.

"Yup. I would have to agree," Steve said.

"Is it possible," I offered, "that the issue may not be so much what you talk about, but how you talk about it?"

As I looked at Steve and Kim, I tried to imagine living in a home with closeness and love one day and hand-to-hand combat the next. How could two people communicate so effectively at work and yet fail so miserably at home?

Is this problem unique to Steve and Kim? Of course not. At some point in their relationship, most couples find themselves facing off against one another.

Polarization

The type of communication plaguing Steve and Kim's relationship is called *polarization*. It occurs when couples takes positions on a topic and then debate it as if it had simple, right and wrong answers. Each partner defends his or her position against the fiercest attacks. They fire shots back and forth in an effort to distract, defeat, or even demolish their partner. They draw lines and wage the war until a victor emerges. We know, however, that no one wins in these battles. They only serve to weaken the love and affection that should be the strengths of a marriage.

Steve and Kim were fighting about his treatment of her daughter, his stepdaughter. It was a round-robin engagement that never ended. She contended that he played favorites.

"You are much harder on Karen than you are on the boys," she said. "When you pick on her so much, it just pushes both of us away from you. You're on her from the time she gets up until she goes to bed at night. You criticize her so much that she thinks you don't love her. No wonder she's rebelling."

"I'm no harder on her than on Jimmy and Todd," he snapped. "When she does something wrong and I discipline her, she runs to you to tell you how badly I've treated her. The boys don't do that. They usually admit that they've done something wrong and accept their punishment. Not Karen."

And so it went for several minutes while I considered how to intervene. These two people had taken positions and were defending them. They were lambasting and vilifying each other, portraying each other in the worst possible light and accusing each other of having unfair motives. Kim accused Steve of disliking Karen; Steve accused Kim of overprotecting and favoring Karen. The assaults continued. The gap widened.

Were they communicating effectively? No.

Could they make any progress if they continued to talk this way to one another? No. Their polarization would only serve to separate them even further and propel them to divorce court.

Steve and Kim sat tensely in the stuffed chairs, gripping the armrests for support as they hurled insults back and forth. I knew, however, that under the surface, both were exhausted from this kind of communication. I could see the sadness in their eyes. I watched Steve anxiously try to defend himself against the barbs Kim delivered. I could see the hurt as Kim tried to protect her daughter. Both were far more fragile than they let on. Both were utterly worn out by the anger that permeated their household. They knew that their marriage was in jeopardy if they didn't find solutions soon.

Where Did It Begin?

Where did all of this blaming and denial and hiding begin? Certainly not with Steve and Kim. It began long ago, in the Garden of Eden.

Adam was created as the first man and given the joys and delicacies of the Garden for his domain. Even with all of these pleasures, God said, "It is not good for man to be alone. I will make a helper suitable for him" (Genesis 2:22).

Most would agree that His choice of a partner was flawless. Woman—the delight of man. God's intent was that man and woman would live in harmony with one another and with Him.

Harmony. Union. These things were in God's heart when He created man and woman. It was an idyllic setup. At their disposal was the lush Garden, filled with every possible fruit. "Trees that were pleasing to the eye and good for food" (Genesis 2:9). Freedom to enjoy the Garden, freedom to tend to the Garden, freedom to live in a land that flowed with water and life. What could possibly go wrong?

Obviously, things went wrong in a big way. The blunder committed by Adam and Eve was enough to rock creation and send the universe spinning out of control for all time.

If you had sat with me, observing Steve and Kim on that troubled morning in my office, you would have seen that the problems that originated with Adam and Eve have not dissipated. If you have watched a wonderful union turn into a terrible battlefield where hearts are torn apart and intimacy and hope are destroyed, you probably agree that things remain terribly amiss.

But what is wrong? What happened?

Genesis 3:7

What happened was this. The man and woman were deliriously happy. Adam waxed poetic in his ecstasy:

> This is now bone of my bones
> and flesh of my flesh;
> she shall be called "woman"
> for she was taken out of man.

These words have been used for generations to express the power of the union between man and woman. Bone of my bones, flesh of my flesh. Can anything be as intimate as this? They were united. At least God created them to be united.

But into this wonderful scene came the wily serpent, who knew what resided in the hearts of Adam and Eve. Man and woman had been given complete freedom to eat of any tree in the Garden except for one. "You are free to eat from any tree in the garden; but you must not eat from the tree of the knowledge of good and evil, for when you eat of it you will surely die" (Genesis 2:16-17).

I can imagine Adam and Eve wondering if God's words were really true. After all, how could everything else in the Garden be blessed while one tree was so horrific? Perhaps God was wrong on this one count.

Do their words not sound a bit like our own? We wonder if we can get away with just this one little sin. Can we push the envelope just this once and get away with it? We all want to test the limits. We learned it from Adam and Eve.

The serpent's temptation hit Adam and Eve where they were most vulnerable. He teased them with the possibility that the one tree that was forbidden was actually the best tree, offering the best fruits. "For God knows," he said, "that when you eat of it your eyes will be opened, and you will be like God, knowing good and evil" (Genesis 3:5).

What a possibility! The opportunity to be like God was too much to pass up. And they didn't pass it up. And the spiral began.

Eve saw that the tree was good for food, pleasing to the eye, and desirable for gaining wisdom. She took fruit from it and ate. The consequences cascaded down upon them and upon us as well.

"Then the eyes of both of them were opened, and they realized they were naked" (Genesis 3:7). They were no longer innocent and protected. The Lord came into the Garden and asked where they were. I suspect God was not merely inquiring about their physical location. He questioned their emotional and spiritual whereabouts. He knew, of course, what had happened. Instead of standing up to answer God, Adam and Eve hid. This marked the beginning of humankind's ongoing dance of deception.

Adam and Eve didn't just hide. When confronted with their shameful actions, they hurled blame at one another. Neither was willing to take responsibility. They pointed fingers, feverishly trying to avert blame.

Sound familiar? Does this also sound like Steve and Kim?

Adam blamed Eve; Eve blamed the serpent. We have been blaming one another ever since in a desperate attempt to avoid guilt and responsibility.

Shame is the feeling that comes from knowing that what we have done is terribly wrong. But it is more than feeling guilty about wrongdoing—it is the horrible realization that we are bad down to our core. While we may frantically try to displace responsibility, most of us know that we have contributed to the mess that we are in.

We know in our hearts that we are fallible. At times, we feel our fragility. We cannot seem to avoid committing destructive acts that break apart relationships. Despite our good intentions, we don't communicate effectively and build strong unions with those that we care about.

Destructive Patterns

What we perceive in Adam and Eve, we find in ourselves. We see it in Steve and Kim as well. We see carefully learned and well-rehearsed traits that create distance and distrust in relationships. We see patterns of communicating passed from generation to generation. These destructive patterns destroy trust and damage our ability to communicate effectively. Thankfully, we can learn new skills to create harmony and trust. Before we do that, however, let's look closer at some unhealthy communication patterns that have entered our lives.

A World of Deception

Scott Peck, in his book *People of the Lie*, suggests that dishonesty is a major problem in relationships and alienates us from one another. Because vulnerability is frightening, we often choose to live behind disguises. We pretend that we think one thing when in fact we may actually believe something entirely different. We tell little half-truths instead of telling the whole truth. Eventually, this creates chaos in a relationship. Willard Harley Jr., in his book *Love Busters*, explains:

> Couples are not only ignorant of methods that can improve their marriages, they are often ignorant of the problems themselves. They deliberately misinform each other as to their feelings, activities, and plans. This not only leads to a withdrawal of love units, when the deception is discovered, it also makes marital conflicts impossible to resolve. As conflicts build, romantic love slips away.[3]

Harley suggests that couples must get off the easy path of deception. Rather than take the tempting road of dishonesty, he recommends that you "reveal to your spouse as much information about yourself as you know: your thoughts, feelings, habits, likes, dislikes, personal history, daily activities, and plans for the future." I would like to add one more: Be honest about your part in any problems. Stop the dance of deception.

A World of One-Upmanship

Many of us, especially men, tend to compete with one another, and our communication reflects that. Rather than trying to understand one another, we try to gain an advantage. The deception in this kind of maneuvering is clear. Often we go against deeply held values to serve other motives. In order to win, we compromise what we believe.

Deborah Tannen, author of the bestseller *You Just Don't Understand,* says that many men tend to live in either a one-up or one-down world with hierarchical social order. "In this world," she says, "conversations are negotiations in which people try to achieve the upper hand if they can, and protect themselves from others' attempts to put them down and push them around. Life, then, is a contest, a struggle to preserve independence and avoid failure."[4]

In their insightful book, *The Art of Possibility,* authors Rosamund Stone Zander and Benjamin Zander share a story of a competitive business relationship. They describe two men who tried to work out a business deal but came to an impasse. On the surface, both wanted to make the deal work, but there was so much ego involved—or what the authors call the "calculating self"—that progress in negotiations came to a standstill. Beneath the surface, each man was hostile, controlling, and seeking a "win" on his own terms. The softer side of their personalities—the "central self"—was stuck. Too much energy was being used to gain supremacy over the other person, so cooperation could not really take place. Passive-aggressive energy ruled the day.

The Zanders note, "Since the calculating self is designed to look out for Number One, we are likely to find it in the driver's seat when there is an impasse, whether in politics or personal relationships."[5] They explain that plotting to win always pulls the conversation into a downward spiral.

You may recall the immense popularity of Steven Covey's books, including *The Seven Habits of Highly Effective People.* He too recognized the manipulative, controlling self as a major culprit in unhealthy relationships. He said that for effective communication to take place, we must first seek to understand, rather than to be understood. Of course, this goes against our natural tendency.

What is it like to be in a relationship with someone who must win each round of conversation? This was the case for Steve and Kim. Each fought to gain control of the conversation, attempting to persuade the other of his or her "right" point of view. In this scenario, both participants believe that one wins and one loses. Of course, we know that both ultimately lose.

A World of Blame

We often refuse to take responsibility for our actions. Instead of speaking the truth to one another and taking personal responsibility, we often dance our way around issues. Instead of having a godly sorrow that leads to repentance (see 2 Corinthians 7:10), we shift the blame whenever possible. Needless to say, we rarely settle issues in this environment.

Watching Adam and Eve squirm must have been somewhat humorous for God. Can you picture the scene? He had caught our ancestors in the act. He knew what they had done, and they knew what they had done. There they were, naked and ashamed. Yet when He confronted them, they tried to divert attention from their deceitful act (the first major cover-up in history). The man and the woman pointed their fingers in every direction except back at themselves. They used blame, denial, justification...anything that could possibly dilute their own guilt. It was something akin to catching your three-year-old son with his hand in the cookie jar and him saying he wasn't to blame; the jar had fallen off the shelf onto his hands. Though pathetic, our efforts to avoid the truth are somewhat amusing.

When blame enters the relational world, however, the humor vanishes. Instead of sitting honestly with his spouse, admitting culpability and then seeking forgiveness and making amends, the artful dodger blames others. Problems are always someone else's fault. The intricate web of deception continues to grow, and solving the problem becomes increasingly difficult.

A World of Confounded Communication

When rampant blame and protracted explanations interfere with honest communication, chaos reigns. That is why, after a particularly heated fight in your marriage, one of you looks to the other and asks, "What were we arguing about?" The issues become so cloaked in accusation, innuendo, blame, and rationalization that the real issues are forgotten. People get caught up in the fever of the battle. "Win, win, win," the little voice in our head shouts.

A glance back at the conversation between Steve and Kim shows how handily he deflects her desire to communicate. After a quick jab, pointing out Karen's manipulations and how Kim favors her daughter, he shifts the topic to dinner reservations. Can you imagine Kim's confusion when he does this?

Again, I can picture God listening to Adam's windy explanations and then listening to Eve go on and on about the serpent. It is psychobabble at its best, nothing more than abject nonsense.

A World of Coercive Communication

Communication, in this kind of relationship, is not a way to truly understand one another. Communication is used to outwit others, manipulate them, or make them feel stupid so that they will back down. This pattern fits both sexes, but I think that men are particularly guilty of maneuvering conversation to get what they want. Because of their competitive bent, coercive communication comes easily to them. Have you felt it? Can you recall a time in your marriage when your spouse tried to convince you of how wrong you were when you weren't even discussing a right-or-wrong issue?

Consider another couple with whom I worked recently.

When Jan and David came to see me, they made it clear from the outset that they expected me to be an arbiter. They had firmly entrenched ideas about how things ought to be, and finding themselves at an impasse, thought they would seek out an "expert" who would declare one of them the victor. I could see that such an arrangement would not help them and would make me a hero to one and a villain to the other. I didn't want any part of that proposition.

It seemed that David wanted to be able to go back to college to earn a bachelor's degree. No problem so far. In fact, this seemed like an admirable goal. He said that he wanted to do this for his family so that Jan might be able to cut back on work to stay home with their three young children. Still no problem, at least with his motive. I wondered, *Why did Jan oppose this plan?* She explained that she did not want to take out a loan for his schooling. She also thought the timing was bad. With a young family, he was already often away from home because of his demanding job as a loan officer at a local bank.

What became interesting as Jan and David talked this out was not the conflict but rather how heated it became and the way that they fought about it. As was the case with Steve and Kim, both people were talking, but nobody was listening. Each had created a tightly woven rationale for why his or her point of view was right and why the other's was wrong. Then, in step-by-step fashion, they used coercion to try to unravel the other's decision.

I listened to their verbal volleys. David shared how reasonable it was for him to go back to college now while the children were young. They would be in school while he worked, and he would only be attending classes two nights a week. As for the money, he would receive a low-interest loan from his own bank to pay for it. How could he pass up a deal like that?

Easy, Jan surmised. She believed that David was not going back to school for the family at all but for his own selfish motives. She had repeatedly told him how his actions would adversely affect the family. This was hard to prove or disprove, of course. She reasoned that though he might only be gone two nights a week, his studies would take him away from family activities for much of the week. Good point, I thought. Finally, low interest or not, the loan still meant more debt, and she did not like the idea of taking on more than they already had.

The lines had been drawn, battle plans were in place, and the war was in progress. Now they wanted me to determine the victor, which I would not do. My work with them, and with so many other couples, is to help them see that they need not engage in warfare to win. Their task was much more difficult. They needed to listen to one another and find solutions that would be acceptable to both of them. They needed the tools that will be offered in this book far more than they needed any quick answer I could render.

A World of Prideful, Protective Communication

We are reluctant to communicate in a way that reveals our deepest needs and fears. Even if we are willing to own responsibility for our part in a problem and to speak without overt deception, too often we communicate from the head, not from the heart.

Most of us would readily admit that we read about communication because we want a more intimate relationship with our spouse. But we want closeness without vulnerability. We want the warmth of attachment without the cost of revealing our deepest nature. Cheap love, I call it. It's not that easy. We cannot have one without the other. We must learn to share from our hearts, not just our heads. We must come to understand our inner emotions, not just what we think about things. Then we can share our entire selves with our partner.

In his mid-century classic *The Art of Loving,* Erich Fromm shares some insights about love. He says that despite all the talk about love and the deep desire to have love, we are poor lovers. Instead of putting our energies into loving one another, we tend to put our energies into attaining success, prestige, money, and power. His words have the sting of conviction.[6]

Men, Communication, and You

You have probably correctly surmised that many men are more regressed in the art of communication than women. However, this does not mean that women should assume their communication skills are polished and effective. Women certainly know how to talk. But do you know how to really communicate with your man?

You have picked up this book because you are looking for a way into the psyche and heart of your man. Your efforts will not be in vain. But why, you may be wondering, do you have to work so hard to communicate with him while he gets let off the hook?

Men do not generally beat down the door to their local marriage counselor or pastor in order to enhance their communication skills. Women are far more active in working on relational issues. For many reasons, men have been trained and enabled to keep their emotional heads in the sand and leave the relational work to the women. Right or not, this is how it has been. That is why I wrote this book: to empower you to change the patterns of communication with your man.

In a recent book of mine, *Does Your Man Have the Blues?* I wrote extensively about how men are typically underdeveloped. More than women, men tend to rely on the ineffective communication tactics I've listed. They have been taught to keep their feelings hidden, to be tough, to buck up under it all, and to never (and I mean *never!*) show vulnerability. And that often means never going to a counselor or admitting that their life is not working.

Men, perhaps because of their lack of intimate communication, often do a fair amount of work around the house. They incorrectly assume that what they *do* for their wives will tell them that they love them. Men work long hours, maintain the cars, and mow the lawn, and they often believe that ought to be enough. Why must they share all that touchy-feely stuff, they wonder? Do they really have to listen? Many men have sacrificed their lives on the altar of work, only to have their wife leave because he wouldn't take the time to sit and talk with her.

Still, wailing about men's shortcomings does no good. Male bashing is passé and not particularly useful. Rather, you can examine how you are communicating with your man, evaluate what is working and what is not working, and learn more effective skills. I think some of the material in this book may surprise you because it reveals that some of the things you are doing actually create barriers between you and your husband.

Although the process will be difficult, this book will help you overcome those communication barriers. Together, we will find ways to share effectively and teach him to share effectively too.

An Opportunity for Women

The bad news is that the world was given a swift blow to our underbellies by Satan and by humankind's sinful response to God's goodness. Separation from God carried consequences for each of us.

The good news, and there is plenty, is that we have the power of Christ to enlighten and strengthen us to overcome these negative traits.

The good news is that we can learn more effective methods of communication.

The good news is that we have an opportunity to assist men to become effective communicators.

This book will help you learn new ways of sharing your needs so that your man will actually listen to you. Remember that God said in the beginning that it was not good for man to be alone. Remember also that He said He would create a help-mate for man. Well, here's your chance—not only to learn to communicate effectively so that your needs are met, but also to teach him more effective skills in the process. It's a win-win proposition.

In an exciting book titled *The Men We Never Knew,* Daphne Rose Kingma says that men cannot save themselves from their emotional-relational difficulties and that women are designed to assist them in this task.

> Women are brought inescapably to this task because men don't have what they need to do it for them-selves....Men are also hobbled in whatever efforts they might put forth because, unlike women, they have neither the emotional experience nor the history of emotional supportiveness that would enable them to evoke the missing feminine in one another....Al-though the task may seem overwhelming, women are better equipped than ever before for this Herculean undertaking.[7]

You have a wonderful capacity for empathizing with your man. You understand love; you know the importance of com-munication. You have been created to be relational in nature, and your man needs your help. Consider this a profound oppor-tunity to help him develop effective communication and inti-macy skills. If he does not learn these skills in his marriage, he will likely not learn them at all.

Are you ready to gain his attention in a new, more mean-ingful way? Are you ready to escort him into a deeper, more pro-found manner of relating? This book will provide you with many opportunities to learn effective tools for communicating with your man—tools that have been proven to be effective.

First Things First

Perfect communication between man and woman was not the only thing harmed in the Garden. Communion with God was also damaged. Each of us needs to repair that relationship. Thankfully, Christ has created a way for us to reestablish harmony with God, and you will need to call on His strength when you work on your relationship with your man.

We must be clear from the onset that any effort to change how you relate to your man will be enhanced if you first commit your relationship to God. The Scriptures are clear about the opportunity to be close to God and the benefits that will accompany that bond. We have many promises:

- He wants us to pray to Him (1 Timothy 2:8).
- He can sympathize with us, for He has been tempted in every way that we have been (Hebrews 4:15).
- We can approach the throne of grace with confidence (Hebrews 4:16).
- We are children of God through faith in Christ (Galatians 3:26).
- Because we have been justified through faith, we can have peace with God (Romans 5:1).
- God works for the good of those who love Him (Romans 8:28).
- He comforts us in our troubles so that we can comfort others (2 Corinthians 1:3-4).

So, friend, I ask you to risk looking at your situation with new eyes. I ask you to see the task ahead as an opportunity, a challenge designed by the Creator. He gave you the opportunity to be a "helpmate," and opening the door to effective communication is certainly one way you can help.

I also ask you to enter into an agreement with God that you will first seek a relationship with Him. Restore your communication with Him, and the other things you desire will soon be added to your marriage.

Two

What's He Hearing?

*Honest disagreement is often
a good sign of progress.*

MAHATMA GANDHI

I watched in dismay as a young mother tried to manage her four-year-old son in the waiting room of my office.

"What is your jacket doing on the floor?" she asked impatiently. "What have I taught you? And why aren't you picking it up? Why are you ignoring me?"

Her questions came like a spray of gunfire. She hovered over her son as if he were committing an incredibly egregious act. My secretaries soon were distracted from their work. They looked at me and then at the mother and child. The mother's voice grew louder with each question.

I wondered what the boy was hearing. What was going on in his young mind? Perhaps this is the way he perceived things:

"What is your jacket doing on the floor?"

"Huh? I don't get it. My jacket isn't doing anything. It's just sitting there."

"Why aren't you picking it up?"

"But Mom, you never told me to pick it up. You asked me what my jacket was doing on the floor."

"Why are you ignoring me?"

"I'm not ignoring you. I just don't understand you. I'm trying to follow your questions, but they're coming at me so fast that I don't have a whole lot of time to think."

I made up his responses, of course. But not the scene. In all too many homes, parents have similar conversations with their children. Perhaps you recognize that you talk this way at times to your children—or your man.

What strikes me most about the "dialogue" between this mother and child is that the conversation is really not a conversation at all. It is one exasperated person sharing her frustrations in a way that fails to achieve the desired results.

It clearly is not a meaningful sharing between two people. Unfortunately, however, it is all too typical of conversations we have with others—including our spouses. Now is the time to bring clarity, relevance, and power to our conversations.

Conflict Happens!

In the situation between the mother and child, we see something common in many shared experiences: two wills in opposition. The mother wants the child to obey immediately, but the child has another agenda. The same is certainly true of adult relationships—perhaps even more so. Two different people, from different backgrounds, with different experiences and expectations, try to reach an agreement. They don't always succeed, and conflict is the result. Because of this, we should identify some truths about conflict in communication.

Conflict happens. We can't get around it. If you are in an honest relationship, you will have disagreements. If you are privileged to be with someone who speaks his mind, you will have tension. The issue is not whether there will be conflict but how you will deal with it. Because conflict is inevitable, we must work on the following practical steps for dealing with it.

One, *normalize it.* Because conflict is unavoidable, don't turn it into a catastrophe when it occurs. Conflict does not signal the end of the world, nor of the relationship. Conflict does not mean the marriage is over. In fact, quite the opposite. An honest encounter may have just begun, and that is a powerful starting point for a meaningful relationship.

Two, *expect it.* Anticipate conflict and treat it as part of the relational package. It is part and parcel of your marriage. You cannot have the sweetness of romantic love without the saltiness of tension at times. In fact, it is best to not label conflict as bad. It is part of a relationship.

Three, *prepare for it.* Talk to your man about issues ahead of time, not just when things are heated. If you develop an understanding that conflict will happen, disagreements will not take you by surprise. Know how you will answer when they come.

Four, *rehearse it.* Develop a strategy for how you will listen to each other and how you will address the issues. Don't simply rehearse the conflict, however. Rehearse solving problems effectively. Practice does not make perfect; perfect practice makes perfect. The same is true with conflict. You will need to rehearse communication tools to become effective problem solvers.

Five, *lighten it.* In order to manage the conflict in your marriage effectively, recognize the absurdity of it. This is very hard when you are in the middle of a struggle, but later you can sit with your spouse and discuss how silly some of your fights have been. You can agree to lighten things up next time you feel the situation begin to get heated. A wink or a smile from your spouse—perhaps a signal to "chill out" when things begin to intensify—can lighten and defuse the situation.

Cranor Graves, author of the book *Building a Marriage*, explains that conflict is a normal part of any enduring relationship. "When couples report to me that they never have conflicts, I feel regret. Is one of them not thinking? Are they sweeping everything under the rug? How dull their life must be. Conflict is not only inevitable, it is also desirable."[1] He offers several specific suggestions for handling conflict.

- Stick to the present.
- Attack the issue, not the partner.
- Listen to each other carefully.
- Refrain from name-calling.
- Refrain from judging motives.
- Avoid "you always" and "you never."
- Do not compare one another with others.[2]

A Reticent President

Mary Todd's friends knew her as a "pretty talker." She had a quick wit and often led conversations. Sharing came easily to her. Her spark and vivaciousness were magnetic to many men. Who doesn't like a woman who can hold her own in a conversation, is conversant on many topics, and can entertain others with ease? Add to that an ability to supply a speedy comeback to those that might challenge her, and we can easily understand Mary Todd's charisma.

Mary is described by writer Ruth Painter Randall as having a "vivid face which dimpled or frowned in tune with the needs of her story, with a rare gift of mimicry, with enthusiasm that brought out all the color in what she was telling, she could hold a roomful of people in rapt attention. She loved people, was intensely sociable."[3]

Young Mary, as she was called, was a popular young woman. She was friendly, responsive, and outgoing. She could have found a man who would reach out to her, engage emotionally with her, and hold lengthy conversations. She could have sought someone who would sit with her when she was feeling distraught. But she sought something different. Sometimes, opposites really do attract. She was interested in a young man named Abraham Lincoln. She was attracted to his bright mind, his political aspirations, and his stability. What do we know about Abraham Lincoln's conversational abilities? Some historians have said that he struggled to hold a lengthy tête-à-tête with a woman because he did not understand the feminine mind. (Nothing new there!) He struggled with low self-esteem and disliked his appearance. He was considered a very plain-looking man.

People are complex, and Lincoln was no exception. He struggled to share his emotions, but he was able to talk about "feminine" matters through poetry. Both he and Mary loved verse, wrote some themselves, and had many conversations about the topic and other aspects of literature. This common ground bridged the gap between their personalities. Would their similarities be enough to hold them together? History has presented differing portrayals about their relationship.

Lincoln apparently disliked talking about trivial matters, but he clearly had a keen mind and massive intellectual powers. His ability to discern critical issues and expound upon them is a matter of history. Mary was "always ready to listen to talk of politics and when it came to that subject the young lawyer was in his element. He may have had a certain social awkwardness but when he had given in Springfield his Lyceum address on political institutions the year before he met Mary, it had been no commonplace speech."[4]

Abraham Lincoln was clearly destined for fame and power. He had incredible tenacity and was determined to succeed. However, he also suffered from bouts of depression and had difficulty sitting down and chatting with his wife. His dark moods, along with his discomfort with the softer side of life, led to marital challenges similar to those that many women face today.

If someone as brilliant as President Lincoln had trouble sharing his heart, what hope do the rest of us have? If anyone could overcome personality hurdles, surely the man who wrote the Emancipation Proclamation could.

What is going on inside the minds of men?

"We Can't Seem to Talk"

Recently, I met with a couple who had been married only six months. John and Kathy are in their forties, and both have been married twice before. They bring to their marriage a lot of hurt and distrust as carryovers from their previous relationships. They also feel some humiliation for trying counseling after already experiencing two failed marriages. They think, as many of us do, that they should have this "communication thing" down by this point in their lives. However, as we can all attest, effective communication can be unbelievably difficult at any stage of life.

And now this newlywed couple sits in front of me and, after having been married only six months, announces that they are already separated. *Yikes*, I say to myself. I know that relationships are difficult, but how can a couple fall so far in such a short period of time?

John and Kathy shared an all too familiar story. Perhaps you can relate.

"We can't seem to talk," Kathy said. "I can't take the silences anymore. He won't talk. I'm ready for some honest communication so we can get back together, but he refuses to talk to me. I wait for him to address some of our problems, but he can't get past small talk. I don't know what to do."

"What is your take on the situation, John?" I asked. I watched as he hesitated. He stroked his black goatee, as he glared at Kathy in obvious annoyance.

Kathy is a pretty woman, but she is quite overweight. Her hair was pulled back in a ponytail. She was not smiling and seemed quite reserved in this first session with me. She returned John's glare.

"I don't talk to you because you are not easy to talk to," John said sharply. "You want to blame me for everything. I'm your husband, but I feel like you don't even like me. Why would I want to talk about things when I know I am just going to be bombarded with questions and accusations?"

The next few minutes were awkward. John and Kathy were both obviously in a lot of pain. Both felt hurt and angry and could not find a way to talk without getting upset with one another. I watched each flinch under the other's verbal assault. I could almost see the wall growing between them. They would not develop intimacy until they learned to communicate more effectively.

Communication inevitably leads to conflict. Intense differences of opinion should not surprise or alarm us. The critical issue is *how* we argue—how we share our viewpoints and listen to each other, how we explore possibilities and how our arguments end. Couples who are able to find win-win resolutions to their conflicts fare much better than those who leave conflicts hanging.

Thinking about that analysis, I encouraged John and Kathy to slow down and pay attention to how they talked to one another. Rather than get into particular issues, I encouraged them to look closely at the way they communicated. I told them that they needed to change the way they talked so that they could resolve issues instead of hurting and discouraging each other with heated exchanges. I wanted them to see that ongoing conflict drains the life out of a relationship and that they really could resolve their issues.

Genesis 3 Revisited

I often see the results of what happened so long ago to set the relational world on its ear. Let's review what turned a world of closeness, vulnerability, and intimacy into one of barriers, walls, and distance.

You remember that after Adam and Eve made their fateful choice, they tried a series of deceptive maneuvers. When God confronted them, Adam was the first to pass the buck.

"It was all her fault," he said.

"No, it was the serpent's fault," she replied.

Ever since that day, men and women have struggled to establish intimacy. Ever since, they have hurled blame at one another, struggling to truly communicate. Ever since, men have tended to hide from their truest emotions and seek solace in their work and other distractions.

The cascade of events resulting from Genesis 3 cannot be overstated. The idyllic setting of Eden has been replaced by a world rife with agony. Ours is a world of unrest. It is a world of personal, local, national, and global conflict. Neighbors fight with neighbors, nations fight with nations, and spouses fight with each other. Every day we read of more soldiers and civilians killed in war, and we also read of blood shed between intimate partners over seemingly trivial matters. Acrimony. Hostility. Conflict. They seem inescapable.

God warned of the disaster that would occur if we disobeyed, but He still called His creation good. He still made us in His image, and we still bear a flawed version of that image. We are still capable, by God's grace, of doing good. God knew that disobedience would affect humankind in a terrible way. He knew that nations would war against nations. He knew that relationships and marriages would face difficult challenges.

The apostle Paul warned the immature Christians at Corinth that marriage was not for everyone and that some people should remain single so that their love for the Lord would not be divided. He knew that marriage can be taxing and requires extra effort to remain emotionally healthy (1 Corinthians 7:1-7,26-40).

Men Are Clams!

In the midst of this troubled world, Kathy and John are trying to resist the tide of divorce and create a loving relationship, but the force working against them seems too powerful at times. They feel discouraged. Perhaps you know exactly how they are feeling.

Kathy wants John to share his heart with her. She wants him to tell her how important she is to him. She wants to be cherished—something all women want. But what is going on inside her man and so many other men? Let's take a closer look.

Dr. David Clarke, author of *Men Are Clams, Women Are Crowbars* (even more disparate than Venus and Mars!), has a lot to say about what is happening inside men like John as women like Kathy try to get through to them.

Clarke has a great deal of empathy for women trying to communicate with men. In the introduction to his book, after noting a litany of differences that tend to push couples apart, he says this:

> The real capper for women is their frustrated attempts to engage men in deep, personal conversations. Men aren't very good at deep, personal conversations. It seems to women that all men think about is food, their jobs, sports, and sex—not necessarily in that order. Men don't talk much, and when they do open their mouths it's to belch or ask you to pass the mustard.[5]

This is a scathing commentary about men. Is it accurate? Well, at least partially.

Does it hurt? Of course.

Is this the problem that we need to address in this book? No.

While many authors focus almost entirely on the differences between men and women and are convinced that these differences are the problems that need to be addressed, I take a slightly different tack. It is this: *Men and women do relate differently, but women can use strategies to effectively communicate with men.*

But let's get back to the issue of men being clams, which has at least some truth to it. John was strong and quiet with rugged good looks. I could see why Kathy was attracted to him. However, she described him as controlling, a claim that I suspect had more than a kernel of truth to it. He guarded what he said in the session. He was careful with his words. Was that part of his control? Perhaps.

John explained that he had never let anyone get too close too fast. In that respect, he was typical of many men. When he was wounded emotionally, his first response was to pull back. "Hurt me once, shame on you. Hurt me twice, shame on me."

John said that he had been hurt by his father as a child. Not surprisingly, his father had been a rough, tough man who expected a lot from his son. Subsequently, John learned that he could rely only on himself. He grew up knowing that no one would be there to help him deal with painful emotions. That's why he was so uncomfortable when Kathy pushed him to share his feelings. This was foreign to him, as it is to many men.

Yes, John was a clam. Most men are. We men want control over our situation. We run from conversations that contain the potential for too much emotion. We are not comfortable with conflict. In the face of a quarrel, men are inclined to rely on one of two options: fight or flight. Neither works all that well, but that is what we have been taught by our fathers and by our fathers' fathers.

Fight or Flight

In many situations, men choose both—they try flight (avoidance) and may ultimately resort to fight. Both reactions, of course, are extreme.

Picture this scene. We are at a worksite where two carpenters are working on a house. Although they have never been close friends, they have never experienced open conflict. But on this day, tempers flare. Pent-up emotion can no longer be contained.

Man number one becomes annoyed because he believes the other is "slacking on the job." He has been bothered by this for days but hasn't said anything (flight). Finally, in exasperation he blurts out, "What is your problem? Are you on vacation or something?" (fight).

Man number two: "Just keep your nose out of my business and get your own work done!" (fight).

Here we see a typical encounter between two men attempting to deal with anger. The insults spew out after tension has built for some time. They had apparently been avoiding conflict, but now emotion erupts unrestrained. The conflict is not productive, and the relationship is likely to be tense for some time to come.

How does this scene relate to what we are learning about men and how they relate to women? We can draw several conclusions from this encounter:

First, *men are likely to avoid conflict, at least initially.* Men have a strong inclination to avoid tense encounters. We don't like heated situations and will avoid them (flight) whenever possible. Unfortunately, this means that issues tend to stack up and create barriers between us and others.

Second, *when conflict erupts, it is likely to be aggressive rather than assertive.* Men are not skilled in the art of tactful conflict resolution. When conflict and testosterone meet, aggression often results. Pick up any newspaper, and you will undoubtedly read about some man or group of men who have engaged in their own version of *Dirty Harry Meets Rambo* to settle their differences. It is not a pretty sight.

Unfortunately, when tempers rise, so does aggression. Domestic violence is a national epidemic. We are, as a nation, a hostile, angry bunch, ready to protect our turf.

Third, *men rarely do an effective job of sharing their feelings.* Men have never really learned how to deal with their emotions. They seem only to have two feelings they can identify: mad and okay. Anything more sophisticated than that is often beyond their capabilities.

I realize that I am coming dangerously close to male bashing. That is not my intent. But men cannot identify their feelings and, because of that, they cannot access their feelings to help them solve problems. I am not sure women do a whole lot better, but at least they seem to be able to learn the language of feelings. This topic—learning how to use feelings to resolve conflict—is material for another book.

Fourth, *men do not seek effective solutions.* Of all their weaknesses, this is perhaps the most glaring. Men do not resolve problems. They leave issues smoldering, only to erupt in flames at a later time.

So it is with many relationships.

In those that are healthy, partners use effective ways to solve problems. In those that are dysfunctional, partners rehearse the same problems again and again in dark, somber, brooding fashion. They find no solutions; they simply put problems aside to be revisited another day. Men need to develop some more effective skills or strategies for dealing with conflict.

Women Are Crowbars

If men are clams, what are women? Dr. Clarke believes that women are more like crowbars, trying desperately to open up their men. Does this sound familiar? Have you been trying, without success, to pry meaningful responses from your man?

I have to give women a lot of credit. They are relational and try, tirelessly, to get men to communicate. They put out a lot of energy to solve relational problems. They try and pry to get men to open up and share with them. But if you look at your own record of success and failure, you will probably agree that the crowbar approach does not work.

Kathy moves back and forth with John. She dares to come closer in her desperate attempt to save her third marriage. She reflexively protects herself when feeling vulnerable again. She feels defeated, wants to have a godly marriage, but wonders what is not working.

John shares some critical information that is hard for her to swallow. He says that he finds her probing to be critical. He says that she often opens her encounters with a negative comment.

"You're always on the attack. When you start a conversation, it's always about something I've done wrong. Then I fire something back at you, and things blow up. It makes me not want to be around you."

"But I wouldn't be so critical if you would just open up to me. I wouldn't feel so hurt and come at you if you showed that you were interested in saving our marriage."

And so the free-for-all continues, with both partners feeling attacked. Both are on guard for the next onslaught of arrows. Both develop thick skins to keep the darts from sinking in. Intimacy evades them, and their marriage hangs together by a thread.

Kathy is threatening to John. She is verbal—powerfully verbal. This is not unusual. Most women are stronger in the verbal arena than men. This is threatening to men. John hears her requests as attacks and reacts defensively. He hears that he is a failure and, not surprisingly, tries to defend himself. He hears about all the things he has done wrong and wonders if he is loved.

Clarke explains that the crowbar–clam combination doesn't work. But we knew that, didn't we?

You're Working Too Hard

As we look back at the frantic mother in the opening of our chapter, we see several things that don't work for her. She hovers over her child, acting like a drill sergeant. In her commanding, demanding tone, she unintentionally goads little Johnny to fight back. She sets the tone for a battle of the wills, which she is likely to lose.

But even more importantly, she is working too hard. She is too uptight. She has way too much energy and intensity invested in this battle. Her tone, body language, and words scream to the child, "Get ready. This is war. Do you hear me? This is going to be a battle!"

One might think that such a message would make any child cower in fear and stand at attention. But you know children as well as I do. What are they thinking?

Yippee. This is going to be fun. Mom is uptight and ready to freak out. I have power. This is too good to be true.

I am not saying that your 34-year-old husband is thinking the same thing, but I suspect that you are getting similar results. Neither children nor men respond positively to harsh, angry words. That kind of language sounds an alarm that men must fight. And they do.

The encounter between mother and son suggests that she is pushing far too hard. She is in a dither and needs to lighten up. Does she need to back down and let Johnny dump his coat and toys wherever he likes? Certainly not. But she can use other ways to achieve positive results without engaging in a power struggle.

Dr. Clarke shares his experience on this issue.

> Many of you make the mistake of escalating, getting too intense in your efforts to open up the clam. You are determined to get into the clam. After all, it's not just for you. It's in the best interest of the clam. If he stays shut there is no closeness and he slowly dies there. So, like Joan of Arc you swear a blood oath and save the day. You'll beat on that clam and beat on that clam until one day, one beautiful day, he'll open up and all nature will rejoice....If you attack the clam head on, you will go up in flames just like poor old Joan.[6]

The solution, as we will see, does not include increasing your intensity. It does not include attacking your man. Instead, the solution lies in developing skills designed to show respect for your man, which invites him to change.

Appreciating the Differences

With all the differences between men and women, and the potentially enormous struggle of getting him to talk and listen, you may wonder if God really knew what He was doing back in the Garden. What was He thinking? Why would He create one sex that wants intimacy and another that wants...well, sex?

But as I have said, we need not rail about the differences between men and women or scream about men's inability to learn to listen to your deepest needs. Rather than take this negative, nay-saying approach, I prefer to think that God had a positive point of view. God knows all things, and He is for us, not against us. I cannot imagine that He set us up to be in complete conflict with one another. I cannot imagine that He smirks when couples miscommunicate or that He believes that couples will forever be adversarial, always facing off with one another on the rocky road to intimacy.

No, we can view our relationships from a different perspective. Consider these facts:

First, *God knew that we would need one another to find completion.* Yes, I know this counsel flies in the face of New Age gurus who tout that we should be complete in ourselves. I myself have said similar things at times. We should not look to another to *make us happy,* but God knew that our partner would help us find true joy in life.

Second, *God designed us so that it was not good for man to be alone.* He created us for relationship. The Scriptures weave a fabric of relationships. We can and should enjoy solitude, but God designed us to enjoy one another. God even compares His relationship to us to a bridegroom's relationship to a bride.

Third, *marriage is designed to help us complement one another.* Certainly you have discovered by now that opposites attract, or, at the least, our differences challenge us to become whole people. The extrovert helps the introvert come out of his shell. The introvert helps the extrovert appreciate quiet moments. One partner helps the other save money; the other helps the first loosen up and enjoy life. In a nutshell, differences help us grow.

Finally, *we are designed to rely upon God.* Anyone who has been married or been involved in a long-term relationship knows that things are not easy at times. Relationships include conflict and struggle. The Scriptures tell us that we will have times of difficulty, and those times come not only to test our faith but also so that we might comfort others in their times of trial (2 Corinthians 1:4).

Pick Up a New Tool

We have now set the stage to dig in and start learning new skills. You will need a new tool bag with plenty of room for new tools. Keep in mind, however, that you cannot fill your toolkit with new tools until you have emptied it of the old, rusty, useless ones. You might be a bit attached to those old tools, regardless of how ineffective they are. It is human nature to attach ourselves to our practiced ways of relating. Lightening our load can be tough, even if we know it is for our own good. Do it anyway!

Hopefully, we agree that men have a tough time relating intimately to women. You can sympathize with his difficulties, but he must step up to the plate and learn how to play the game. He must learn how to listen to you, and, with new skills, you will be able to increase the likelihood of that happening.

So I invite you again to put down your old ways of trying to change him. Set aside worn-out temptations to yell at him, scold him, or even threaten him. Put away your desires to call him names, put him down, or compare him unfavorably to certain animals. No manipulating, no pouting, no withdrawing into silence. None of those things work. Let's move forward to learning a new mind-set and a creative set of skills that will revolutionize your marriage.

THREE

Getting His Attention

*Where your treasure is,
there your heart will be also.*

MATTHEW 6:21

⚜ ⚜ ⚜

The room was eerily quiet. Moments before, it had been consumed with a burst of energy, excitement, and panic—a flurry of activity, with doctors shouting orders. Now all was silent.

All eyes were on him. The most beautiful baby boy one could imagine—at least in my mind. My firstborn. A son. His eyes were bright and blue. His skin glowed pink; deep red veins and capillaries were visible just beneath the surface. His body pulsated with life.

He had been a planned child. Lamazed. A labor of love. Everything in the delivery room had been orchestrated to create the optimal environment to birth him into this world. After his abrupt arrival, which was accompanied by screams that let us know his lungs were functioning effectively, I gave him his first bath.

I softly washed the warm water over his skin. He was back in the safe, enveloping liquid he had known for so long. He immediately calmed, and I knew the sensation of oneness, of being both an actor and being acted upon. Time stood still.

47

That attention was just a part of what I invested in my son. I am pleased to report that he has turned out just fine. Joshua is now a 26-year-old medical student and, more importantly, a fine young man. He is caring and honest with a deep Christian faith. Maybe all that attention in the first few moments of his life did add up to something powerful.

Not all focused attention is good, however. Recently, I watched a fellow traveler, seated near me on a jetliner, who was admiring his new purchase—a digital camera. As he scanned the manual for operating instructions, he barely heard the periodic comments from his wife.

"Huh?" he would mumble occasionally, not even calling his wife by name. "Did you say something?"

"Yes, Fred," she said with obvious irritation. "I want to show you something." She pulled out a packet of materials, apparently information about the trip they were taking. He ignored her.

He continued with his task, figuring out how to make this small piece of engineering do what he wanted it to do. He restlessly thumbed through the manual, first looking up the topic in the table of contents and then, when frustrated, switching to the reference material in the back of the book.

I watched as his wife fidgeted. I imagined that she was wondering what to do. She had a round, friendly face with deep lines, suggesting that she had lived a life full of joy and sorrow. Her gray hair hung to her shoulders; her clothes were plain but neat. A middle-class couple, I guessed, in their late fifties or early sixties.

He was also gray, ruffled with a full beard. His glasses were large and dated. I guessed that he had little time or concern for fashion. I assumed that he was a professor, or perhaps an engineer at some software company. He clearly liked his gadgets, but social skills and emotional sensitivity were not obvious strengths.

As he fumbled with the camera, I watched their awkward interaction. She kept trying to get his attention, but he ignored each attempt. She grew more annoyed.

"Why don't you just put that thing away and work on it later? I want to show you something."

"I think I can remember how I did this before. Just give me a couple minutes."

Minutes later she broke the silence.

"Fred! Is it that important? I want to go over our plans with you."

"It seems like it was this setting. I'm just not remembering how it worked before. Do you remember how we did it?"

I watched Fred spend over an hour working up a dither trying to figure out how to operate his camera. He would mutter to himself, "It's supposed to be able to take pictures at a lower resolution. But I can't figure out how it does that. I know I read how to do it somewhere." He would talk to himself and at times, even seemed to answer his own questions. For much of the time, his wife tried, unsuccessfully, to make conversation with him. She finally gave up.

I wondered if they talked like this at home. If so, what kind of relationship did they have? He seemed painfully out of touch with his wife. How did she tolerate his insensitivity? And why didn't she use more effective and assertive strategies to gain his attention?

Fred finally figured out how to make the camera do what he wanted. After he had made it submit to his wishes, he was ready to rejoin his wife.

As I observed this man and his love affair with his camera, I wondered, *Are all men this obsessive? Is it this hard to get our attention? Are we that daft?*

What if we spent this kind of energy and devoted this kind of attention to our marriages and other important relationships? The very attention that we devote to other things could be devoted to deepening relationships. You may need to use this same strategy in order to make the changes you want to see in your marriage. You will have to get his attention, his focused energy, before any substantial change will occur.

This is obviously not a radically new observation. Giving attention to something has always been the first step in significant change. We must first see what we are doing before we can decide to make a change. We must then give the new course of action loving attention to be able to make the requisite adjustments.

Focus. Loving attention. The kind we give to our young children. You will need to focus in order to make the necessary changes in the way you relate to your man. He will need your undivided attention to interact with him in a way that increases the likelihood that he will really listen to you.

Genesis 2:20

Genesis 2:20 contains one of Scripture's most important themes about relationships. God was busy putting creation in order. He wanted everything to be perfect. He had made the heavens and earth, the waters and mountains, and a fabulous garden. Then He made man and gave him the responsibility of naming the animals. Everything was going fine. Then we read, "But..."

But what? "But for Adam no suitable helper was found." God wanted man to have a suitable helper. He wanted everything to be just right. So He formed woman out of man: "Bone of my bones and flesh of my flesh." Though naked, they felt no shame.

In Genesis we see God's attention focused on creating an ideal world, where relationships would function perfectly. No dysfunction hindered this family of God's. He created a perfect man and then created a perfect helpmate, woman.

We are not given much information about this first marriage, but I can imagine that both Adam and Eve worked together as perfect helpmates. I can imagine that they enjoyed perfect communion with each other and with God. I can imagine relationships that were encouraging, supportive, satisfying.

Adam and Eve anjoyed perfect intimacy in the Garden. When some Pharisees asked Christ about marriage, He spoke about two people becoming one flesh:

> Haven't you read...that at the beginning the Creator "made them male and female," and said "For this reason a man will leave his father and mother and be united to his wife, and the two will become one flesh"? So they are no longer two, but one. Therefore what God has joined together, let man not separate (Matthew 19:4-6).

Can you sense the focus here? God's attention is focused on His creation; man's attention is focused on his wife; Eve's attention is focused on her husband. No one was preoccupied with the tyranny of the urgent. No one said, "Can't it wait until later?" or, "I'll give you some time tomorrow."

Sadly, Adam and Eve would go on to become distracted. They would turn their eyes from the Creator and His creation to their own selfish desires. Sin would blind them to God and to one another.

Today, we try, through God's grace, to recapture some of what He intended for us. How does God tell us to regain the focus necessary to recreate intimacy? Listen to the words of the apostle Paul:

> Wives, submit to your husbands as to the Lord.... Husbands, love your wives, just as Christ loved the church and gave himself up for her to make her holy, cleansing her by the washing with water through the word, and to present her to himself as a radiant church, without stain or wrinkle or any other blemish, but holy and blameless (Ephesians 5:22-27).

This is the kind of focused attention required in order for change to happen:

- Focus on your partner's needs.
- Focus on the biblical mandate to love, even when doing so is difficult.
- Focus on love for your mate as an expression of love for the Lord.

Remember that change does not happen without focused attention. Too many distractions can take our minds off what we are trying to change.

Attention Deficits

I have the privilege of working with many families, some dealing with young boys with Attention Deficit Hyperactivity Disorder. We have discovered that these brain-altered children actually have difficulty screening out extraneous stimuli, making learning quite difficult and bringing no end of frustration to their parents and teachers. But I have watched these parents masterfully practice a technique to get their children's complete attention.

Recently, I observed a mother effortlessly manage her ADHD child. When he initially ignored her instructions, she gently followed a series of steps that effectively assisted him to alter his behavior.

First, she gently took him by the shoulders and made eye contact. She knew that without eye contact she could not move forward in their conversation. She kindly asked him to look at her eyes and waited for him to do so before moving forward.

Second, she offered the instruction. She told him specifically what she wanted him to do, reminding him that there was a rule for the behavior she expected. In this case she simply said, "Remember, Zach, we put away one toy before we take others out."

Third, she had the child repeat the instruction. Zach calmly told his mother that he was to put away one toy before he took out another.

Because Zach's mother has repeated this strategy day after day, week after week, his behavior has improved dramatically.

Now let's think about what she did not do. She avoided all these unpleasant behaviors:

- screaming at him
- belittling him
- giving inconsistent messages
- using physical punishment
- doing the task for him

The parallels of this story are quite obvious. We can easily see the need to get the attention of the person you want to impact.

Please Listen to Me

Before the mother could deliver the message to her son, she had to gain eye contact and thereby gain his attention. This may seem like an obvious first step, but it can sometimes be the hardest. Getting the attention of your man may, in fact, be the greatest obstacle in getting him to take you seriously and listen to you.

Listen to what noted author and psychologist Sam Keen has to say about the importance of attention in his book *To Love and Be Loved.*

> Initially, perception is a relatively passive process. A daffodil or a smiling face seizes our attention. We are drawn to a beautiful sunset in the same way that we "fall" for a winsome man or woman. But very quickly we are faced with a decision about where we will invest our consciousness....Once our attention

is captured, a love story develops only if we escalate the contact by a decision to pay attention.[1]

He goes on to share even more about paying attention, that act of tuning in to another, which is so necessary for any kind of relationship to develop, or perhaps more importantly, to be maintained. Focus does not necessarily come easily or naturally. It costs us something.

> Awareness involves willpower and choice. Inevitably I must pay attention to something—baseball, Bach or Barbara. Consciousness is like a flashlight that I choose to focus in a narrow or diffused beam....The price of lasting love is continuing to pay attention to a person, a place, or a work that has become familiar. Paying attention is the bedrock opposite of taking for granted, which is a major cause of death of long relationships.[2]

I find Keen's observation insightful and essential. It seems so simple and yet so profound. I have found his words to be true in my own life.

A few years ago I went through a restless phase with my work. I had been a clinician for more than 20 years, and much of my initial enthusiasm for the work had disappeared. I was understandably troubled by this occurrence. I had always vowed that if the work lost its meaning and energy for me I would find some other vocation. I mulled over the possibility of finding a different job. I wondered about getting more training so that I could move into a different aspect of psychology. I even considered moving into a different kind of work entirely.

As part of my journey, I sought spiritual direction at a renewal center. In a weekend away from family and responsibilities, I let myself sink into my restlessness and ennui. In my simple room, I rested, journaled, and prayed. With my spiritual director I talked about my daydreams of doing something different. We explored how out of touch I was with parts of my work. We talked about how distracted I was, how busy I had become, and how I wasn't paying attention to my work and the people I was trying to help.

I expected the nun to help me explore the possibility of a new vocation. She was wise enough not to do that. Rather, she suggested that I focus my energies even more on the people I was working with. "Notice more, not less," she counseled. "Tune in more, not less. Offer them your undivided attention and see what comes up."

I followed her directions, and though I experienced no earth-shattering revelations, gradually, ever so gradually, my interest in my work returned. I rediscovered the joys of working with people who entrusted me with their secrets, joys, and hopes. Attention to people helped me to find ways of making my work rewarding again. Attention helped me recognize that I prefer to work with certain kinds of problems and not others. Attention helped me read my energy level more effectively so that I was better able to channel my efforts. In short, attention helped.

Getting his attention, in a loving way, is a critical issue. As you begin by focusing on him and telling him about the importance of the relationship, you give him the message that a shared relationship is of utmost value to you. It is an important starting place.

Stopping Time

When you succeed in getting his attention, you will have his time as well. To be fully present requires that he give you his attention and his time. When this occurs, he is fully attending to you. You want not only his time but also the feeling that time has actually stopped. In New Testament Greek, this kind of time is called *kairos* (literally, the fullness of time).

You have undoubtedly experienced what the Greeks called *chronos* time with him—literal minutes or hours of time. With *chronos* time, he promises to spend the evening with you. However, you may be keenly aware that your time together is anything but satisfying. It is shallow, weak, and tepid. He has not given you his undivided attention and is probably easily distracted by work, sports, or other activities.

In *kairos* time, both he and you have a sense of timelessness. You are caught up in being with one another, and time flies. Keen gives us some insights into this wonderful expression of time.

> Love exists in a zone so different from ordinary time (nearer to dalliance than efficiency) that it is said to be "eternal." A lover abandons schedules and becomes fully present in the timeless moment to a child, a friend, a stranger. In giving ourselves in a passionate sexual embrace to our dearest one, or in caring for a suffering stranger who needs our compassion, we escape from the relentless march of measured time that carries us anxiously toward our inevitable conclusion—death.[3]

I watched a friend, Jerry, make this transition not long ago. He was working his way up the management ladder in the banking industry when he was unexpectedly demoted back to loan manager, a job he had held years before. After the demotion, which was an incredible blow to his ego, he changed his attitude about a lot of things. He considered a career change, but with the counsel of his wife, decided that was not best for them. When I listened to him reevaluate his life, I saw that the crisis had brought him and his wife to a closer, more intimate relationship.

"I feel a change happening inside me. Of course, I was troubled about the job loss, but it didn't rattle me the way I thought it would, or the way it might have some time ago. I don't feel as frantic about keeping up with the Joneses as I once did. Now, time is more valuable to me than money or accomplishments. I am saddened when I hear about long-term marriages ending because people haven't spent enough time really appreciating one another. I can see that my marriage could have gone that way. It certainly wasn't because of my greatness that Liz and I are still married. But I am slowing down now. I want to spend more time with her. Maybe the job demotion, which gets me off the fast track, will actually be a blessing. I am excited to get to know my wife again. The kids will be leaving home soon, and we'll have more time for one another. We have new adventures planned, and our time together is more valuable than ever."

Listening to Jerry was encouraging. Many men still don't get it, but some are listening and hearing what they need to hear. Fortunately, Jerry got the message in time to save his marriage. He figured out that money, achievements, status, and the litany of other things men frenetically seek don't add up to much at the end of the road. Perhaps Jerry's job loss spurred him into deeper, more reflective thought. It focused his attention on what is most important in life, a clarifying event that is healthy for any of us. Crisis certainly has done that for other men. Difficult times offer us the chance to change *chronos* time into *kairos* time.

Intentionality

Nothing changes without attention and intention. Jerry made a decision to give both to his wife. At a key point in time, Jerry altered his life's direction. To be more accurate, life actually altered his direction, and this resulted in a shift in his thinking. Many times, outside events or people will be the catalysts to spur us into making necessary changes.

And that is where you come in.

Both attention and intention are essential. One without the other is good but insufficient for change. Both are needed for lasting transformation. I use the term *intentionality* here to indicate purposefulness in one's actions. When one is clear about her intention and purpose, other things seem to fall into place. For example, if you are intentional about improving how you communicate with your husband, change will occur. Why?

Because being intentional requires that you set your sights on a particular outcome, and that tends to reinforce other behaviors that will help you succeed.

I am not promoting an element of control or codependency. Not at all. I am not encouraging you to be obsessed with changing him, nor am I encouraging you to pin your entire happiness on his response to your efforts. Rather, I am encouraging you to set the goal of changing how you interact with him, knowing that this will inevitably lead to change in the relationship.

Rick Warren, author of the highly successful book *The Purpose-Driven Life,* certainly believes in living with purpose. He shares in his book how we have been created for a purpose:

> You were born by his purpose and for his purpose... God is not haphazard; he planned it all with great precision. The more physicists, biologists, and other scientists learn about the universe, the better we understand how it is uniquely suited for our existence, custom-made with the exact specifications that make human life possible.[4]

I believe that God has designed us for relationship—with Him, with our spouse, and with others in our immediate circle of influence. He does not desire for us to be in perpetual conflict with those around us. He has created us to live in harmony, and that harmony is available to us. But we must be purposeful about achieving that goal.

Intentionality sets many things in motion. Consider the woman who decides that she will lose 20 pounds through healthy eating. She is focused and determined. If she is truly committed to her goal, this intentionality and focused attention will lead her to do certain things:

- be selective about the foods she buys for her home
- read about healthy foods and their nutritional values
- choose only certain foods that she will eat

- cut out foods that will hinder her from obtaining her goal
- cook healthier foods for herself and family
- join a gym and exercise program that she will maintain long after she has reached her desired goal

Is this woman focused? Yes. Is she intentional about reaching her desired goal? Yes. Will she reach it? We do not know for sure, but her determination and focused attention, certainly increase her chances.

Houston, We Have a Problem

You have picked up this book because you have a problem with your man taking you seriously. Why do I know that? Because it is something I hear about all too frequently. As a man, I am embarrassed to hear so many women exclaim that their spouses just don't get it. In fact, this became the title of a recent book of mine: *Men Just Don't Get It—But They Can.* He doesn't listen to you, and nothing you do seems to help.

You must get his attention—this is obviously a central premise to the book. But how? Here are some practical tools.

First, *carefully choose a time to talk to him.* Timing is, as you know, critical. Sometimes a person seems ready to hear what you have to say, and other times he doesn't.

Joyce Meyer, in her book *Help Me, I'm Married!* says that you must "learn to wait until you sense the presence of God preparing the heart of the person with whom you need to communicate. Timing is extremely important in good communication....We can cause ourselves trouble by not picking the right time to speak."[5]

You may be tempted to launch into the issues when they are burning in your chest, but you know that is not the most prudent action. Meyer says that you should remain silent when...

- you are angry
- you are tired

- you are under unusual duress
- you want to win
- you want to get even or put your mate down

If you are like me, these are the very times when I want to dive into a thorny issue. My defenses are down, I feel irritable, and I'm ready for a fight. Something inside tells me this is not the best time to get into a touchy issue, but because I feel vulnerable and testy, I may not make the wise choice of waiting for a better time to discuss things.

Second, *agree upon a time to talk.* Set a time when you will have no distractions. You may want to have the kids gone for the evening. Perhaps you will hire a sitter and go out to a quiet restaurant. Your focus at this stage is simply to get his attention. Nothing else. Just his attention. Encourage him to look at you. Having him look at you will make you feel secure in his intention to hear you.

Third, *tell him that you have some concerns about your relationship that you will be sharing in future weeks.* You can review them with him at this time if you feel ready to do so. But this initial discussion is simply intended to begin the practice of gaining his attention so you can examine important issues at a later date. You will have been successful if he listens to you, even if you don't make any important changes.

Fourth, *let him know that his attention is important to you and to your relationship with him.* Speak with passion. Let him know that this is an important first step and that you are intent upon making changes in your marriage.

Finally, *share with him your intentions.* Let him know that you intend to practice some communication techniques that will help bring about changes you want to see happen in your marriage. Let him know that you desperately want change and are willing to start with yourself. Let him know that you are going to work on how you talk to him and become a more effective listener as well.

Having done that, you have set the stage for change to happen. Now you have his attention, and you have your intentions. Nothing earth-shattering has changed yet, but your intentions have changed, and that is critical. You have already taken some very important steps. When you picked up this book, you made another giant leap toward having the kind of marriage you dream about. You are putting feet to your faith.

The Seven Cs

In the many years that I have worked with couples, I have noticed that certain skills work to bring about effective communication and intimacy. Conversely, other behaviors bring about detachment, resentment, and distance. Obviously, we want to enhance those skills that create intimacy and alter those behaviors that lead to hostility and distance.

You want what brings about the intimacy that God wants for you and your spouse. You want what was lost in the Garden. You were created to have a joyful relationship with your spouse and with God, and by God's grace you can have it. Here are Seven Cs we will be exploring in future chapters:

- speaking with calmness
- speaking with clarity
- speaking concisely
- speaking with compassion
- speaking consistently
- speaking with conviction
- speaking with conciliation

I must throw one more in for good measure. Some of you may be thinking that you have tried these things with no results. That may be the the case; no one can follow this recipe perfectly. Still, you can add one more powerful ingredient to these seven.

In every relationship, people experience *consequences* for their choices. This is not a bad word; in fact, it is found in the Scriptures (Colossians 3:25 NASB). God allows people to reap what they have sown. Our actions have natural consequences, and we will see how God's natural laws have their effect. Consequences are powerful motivators for change.

Fixing Our Eyes

You undoubtedly want emotional and physical intimacy with your spouse, but something even deeper is also available, something even more wonderful than the intimacy you have known up until now.

Dr. David Clarke, in his book *A Marriage After God's Own Heart,* says this:

> The secret to genuine, lasting intimacy in a relationship is becoming one flesh, spiritually....Spiritual bonding is consistently placing God at the center of your relationship and growing ever closer to Him as a couple. That means that you include God in everything—you invite Him into every nook and cranny of your relationship. It means that your souls come together in the pursuit of God.[6]

You are after his attention, and you want to be focused and purposeful about getting it, but you must not lose sight of the path that will get you there. You must follow the recipe for healthy communication and encourage him to do the same. But you must also maintain your focus on Christ and His power to make changes in your heart.

Have you ever wanted to change some things in your life, but you did not know how? On the other hand, have you ever simply believed, set the wheels in motion, and seen things fall into place? Belief is a powerful thing. Focus and attention are potent principles that bring about change. They eliminate things that would deter us from our desired destination. Like a laser beam, our purposeful attention has a momentous impact. Now we are prepared to get out the recipe for change and watch for powerful results.

Having our goals bathed in prayer and fixing our eyes on our relationship with Christ is sure to bring about wonderful change. Like the apostle Paul, we say, "So we fix our eyes not on what is seen, but on what is unseen. For what is seen is temporary, but what is unseen is eternal" (2 Corinthians 4:18).

Four

Saying It Calmly

The tongue that brings healing is a tree of life,
but a deceitful tongue crushes the spirit.

PROVERBS 15:4

❧ ❀ ☙

I entered the bustling store with more than a bit of trepidation. Around me, people examined various makes and models of cell phones that could not only make calls but also take pictures, play games, and even compute. Some were large, some small, and some even smaller. My eyes began to glaze over, and the phones became indistinguishable. This gadgetry was both intriguing and intimidating. How was I going to articulate what I wanted, decipher what they would tell me, and still be lucid enough to find my car when I walked out the door?

Before going to the store, I called my friend Tom and consulted with him about what kind of phone to buy. I had a million questions. "Digital? Analog? Both? Dual mode? Tri-mode? Flip phone? Do I want a pager built in? What about a phone with the digital camera?"

His answer was not what I had expected.

"David, have you ever purchased a new car?"

"What?" I said a bit irritated. "You know I have." I could imagine his wry smile and the glint in his eye. I waited for a response, but he seemed content to let his question hang in the silence.

"What does buying a car have to do with buying a cell phone?"

"It's the same thing. They've got you. They know how to sell you what you don't need. They speak a language that will confound you. It's hopeless. Just go in there, get your checkbook ready, and get out as fast as you can. It's going to hurt, but if you're prepared for it and have the right mind-set, you can get out with minimal damage. Pain is mandatory, but suffering is optional."

Tom's counsel was not encouraging. I had a vivid memory of my last car purchase, and it was not pleasant. I was already beginning to feel queasy. I had never imagined that purchasing a cell phone would generate a lesson in life.

If I followed Tom's advice, I was simply to brace myself, get on with it, and get it over. I would try to communicate my needs using the few "cellular phone terms" I had practiced and get out with as little damage as possible. But even rehearsal had not prepared me for what transpired.

Fifteen minutes after entering the store—they never have enough sales staff for the volume of people—my turn finally came.

"Next?" the man said gruffly. A tag on his shirt told me his name was Edwin.

"I'm next," I said. I was still hoping, naively, that this would all work out.

"We'll see," he said.

Looking down at the sign-in sheet, he asked me if I was David Hawkins.

"Yes," I said. My resolve to be friendly and try to win him over was dissipating rapidly.

"What can I do for you?"

I said that a customer service representative had told me that I could have a $50 credit toward a new phone, and that he should have a record of it on my account. He quickly scanned his computer. "We don't have any record of a credit on your account. I'm sorry, but you'll have to pay full retail if you want the phone." He stared at me, waiting for my response. What to do now?

I focused on what I had rehearsed: Stay calm. Stay cool. Repeat what you need.

"Listen. I spoke to Deidre yesterday, and she told me I qualified for an upgrade and that I'm entitled to a $50 credit toward a new phone."

Just when I thought things could not possibly get worse, Edwin leaned over the counter and spoke in a sharp, staccato voice. He repeated that he had no record of any message from Deidre. He was in charge. The only question was whether I was willing to pay full price for a phone or not. "Make up your mind," he said. "I have other customers to help."

I was stunned. I have since thought of a thousand rebuttals to offer Edwin. Would you believe that not one of them came to my mind at that moment? Why? Because he caught me off guard. Because I was not prepared for someone to treat me with such disrespect. Because I don't like conflict.

So, in a meek voice, I simply said, "Sorry. I'll take the phone."

Sorry. I'll take the phone! What kind of response was that? I was a grown man, trained in the art of assertive communication. Why would I act like he was doing me a favor?

Although I did not bark back at that moment, I did so many times over the next four or five hours. I called Edwin names; I ridiculed him. I thought vile thoughts and considered vile actions. Why? Because I was hurt.

What happened to me in that store has undoubtedly happened to you at some time in your life. Perhaps you were in a store, at your work, or in your own home. Perhaps you have used the power of words to gain an advantage over someone else. Perhaps you have crafted your verbal abilities so that, like one engaged in a sword fight, you could outmaneuver a stronger opponent.

Edwin's quick, rapier responses had rendered me speechless. He had bested me. I gave in, bowing to his superiority. But his sharp words caused a great deal of damage.

Did Edwin really win? Of course not. He became a lesser man in the process. He lost my respect. In time, he may lose my business. My guess is that he has never thought again about that encounter. I certainly have. I have rehearsed what he said, and what I could have said, many times. I walked away wounded, and you can be sure that I will respond differently to him should we have another encounter.

I also walked away from my brief encounter with Edwin wondering. I wonder if he had a bad day before I even arrived. Does he have problems at home that crept into his work? To a certain extent, his struggles became my struggles. His lack of calm impacted me, and if I am not careful, they will impact how I treat others. Insensitivity and lack of respect for others can harden us slowly, insidiously. We carry our defensiveness into other relationships and lose pieces of our humanity.

James 3

If the apostle James had been in that cellular phone store, I suspect he would have been appalled but not surprised. "This is what I warned against. The tongue can do so much damage. I have seen it a thousand times. One simple word can turn the whole course of a conversation. One insensitive remark can hurt to the bone. I wish people would learn to be careful with what they say."

In one of the most profound sections of Scripture on the power of the tongue, James offers illustrations that make us think about words and the damage they can do.

> When we put bits into the mouths of horses to
> make them obey us, we can turn the whole animal.

Or take ships as an example. Although they are so large and are driven by strong winds, they are steered by a very small rudder wherever the pilot wants to go. Likewise the tongue is a small part of the body, but it makes great boasts. Consider what a great forest is set on fire by a small spark. The tongue is also a fire, a world of evil among the parts of the body. It corrupts the whole person, sets the whole course of his life on fire, and is itself set on fire by hell....No man can tame the tongue. It is a restless evil, full of deadly poison (James 3:3-6,8).

Here we see James offer three examples of the danger of the tongue. First, he gives us the example of a horse having a small bit in its mouth and explains how this bit has the power to turn a strong, stubborn horse in any direction desired.

Like the bit, the tongue is small and powerful and can be very constructive or very destructive. Just as the bit can turn the horse, so too can the tongue alter the course of a person's life.

Next, James shares the analogy of a ship driven by the winds. But the winds do not determine what direction the ship will take. They provide the impetus for movement but not the direction.

As a sailor, albeit a novice, I will never forget the feeling of controlling the tiller, which directs the rudder. With the wind blowing hard, catching in the sails, I feel the tiller shudder in my hand. The weight of the entire boat comes to a focus in the rudder. An almost imperceptible shift of the rudder sends the boat shooting in another direction.

I remember a recent outing on my sailboat with friends. We were moving at about three knots in the waters of South Puget Sound. The conversation was lively. The sun was warm, and soft, billowy clouds offered a grand mosaic to the azure sky.

Suddenly, with little warning, the winds picked up. Gusts out of the north caught the sails, and we moved briskly across the water. We put away our drinks and snacks as the boat began to heel to the command of the winds.

I felt an immediate surge of adrenaline, perhaps even a moment of fear. There is power in the wind. But the skills I had been honing kicked into place, and I grabbed the tiller, maneuvering the boat to harness the power of the wind. We now tacked vigorously at ten to twelve knots—a delightful speed for my boat. My ability to utilize the rudder would determine whether we really sailed or let the wind control us. It all came down to what the captain was able to do with the rudder. Like the rudder, the tongue is capable of harnessing power and using it in positive or negative ways.

Finally, James offers another metaphor. This is one that we in the Northwest know intimately: the forest fire, which can reduce a verdant expanse of green giants to blackened sticks.

Blessed with acre upon acre of Douglas fir, Sitka spruce, and ponderosa pine, we in the Northwest take for granted our green bounty. We look in any direction and see forest. While we have our share of deciduous trees—western maple, oak, elm, and alder—we take pride in the conifers that stay lush and green throughout the year. We prize our evergreens.

But we have been humbled too many times to dismiss the power of fire. As James says, "What a great forest is set on fire by a small spark." A cigarette thrown out a car window destroys thousands of acres of forest. A campfire left unattended spreads with the wind, and countless man-hours are spent trying desperately to contain the fury of the fire. In the end, firefighters are killed, wounded, or exhausted, and the landscape is ravaged. All by a careless spark.

Like the spark, the tongue packs tremendous power. Used carelessly, the tongue can cause incredible damage. You probably have seen the power of the tongue in your relationship with your husband. You have seen how a quick, thoughtless word can ruin an evening. A snide, well-placed barb can send him reeling in quick retreat, thwarting any hope for intimacy.

Preparing for the Talk

My encounter with the cell phone sales representative was spontaneous and unpleasant. We all have those kinds of conversations at times. All we can do is pick up the pieces later and learn as much as possible from the experience. Other conversations, however, have been left on the back burner of our minds. We have had plenty of time to consider what we want to say and how we want to react. Now is the time to deal with them.

You have picked up this book because you and your mate need to have some conversations. Perhaps there are also friends and family members who need to hear what you have been keeping to yourself. But before you can tell them what you think, you need to prepare yourself. Things must be clear in your mind before you share them.

Trish came to see me for counseling after a recent breakup with her boyfriend, Mark, whom she had dated for the past year. She was young, naive, and discouraged about the fact that sharing with her boyfriend had become so difficult.

"I had thought it would be so much easier," she said wistfully. Times had been challenging. She felt that Mark was strong-willed and unbending. Trish did not feel like he respected her points of view. She was convinced that she was slowly losing her identity in the relationship. She considered going back to him but wanted to think things over before making that decision. She shared with me some of the pros and cons of a possible reconciliation.

She described Mark as a "self-made man." He had come out of high school uncertain about his future but decided to follow in his father's footsteps as an electrician. He was willing to work hard as an apprentice and easily passed the tests to become a journeyman. Having completed that hurdle, he had recently started his own company. Things were going well financially, but he worked long hours and seemed impatient with the demands of a relationship.

"It seems like he never listens to me," Trish said. "I try to tell him how rejected I feel, but he is too preoccupied with his own life. Nothing I do or say is as important as what is going on with him. If I have a problem, his is always bigger."

I encouraged her to tell me more.

"Well, Mark is a really nice guy. He is sensitive, in spite of what I have said about him. In the beginning, he would do anything for me. He is a Christian man, and we have enjoyed attending church together."

"Tell me about how you talk to each other."

"We used to share all the time. But like I said, more and more the talk is about how he is doing and less about what is happening with me. It seems like Mark is uncomfortable with my feelings. He is a problem solver. Very practical. He gets upset when he thinks I'm too emotional. He doesn't like it if I start crying or share too much about my feelings. But I can't help it. That's just how I am."

"What about conflict?" I said. "How do you handle it?"

"Well, it seems like we just slip into fighting. I never see it coming. All of a sudden, we're both angry, and before long, we're yelling at each other. We never used to yell, but that has changed. When the fight is over, neither one of us is proud of how we have talked to the other. But we can't seem to stop it. I hate how he yells at me, and I know he hates how I yell at him. We move from being calm and sensitive to being biting and angry in two seconds."

"If you guys decide to get back together, you will need to learn how to deal with conflict in a healthy manner. You'll need to learn more about why things move from calm to careless and about how they move from friendly to caustic."

"Yes, but he needs to learn how to listen to me too."

"I agree. You both need to learn how to really listen to the other."

"He wants to get back together with me. I think I have his attention now. This two months apart has been good for us. He says that he wants to work on the relationship, so that is a good sign. I'd like to see if it can work, but I need to learn some skills before I go back with him."

It is clear that Trish does not feel prepared to really talk to Mark. She also feels caught off guard by his inability to truly listen to her. They slip into heated conflicts without noticing how it happens. Trish needs to prepare to have a serious conversation with Mark—one that he will hear, one that will lead to healthy choices. But how can Trish prepare for this conversation and others that will undoubtedly occur in the future?

Drs. John Townsend and Henry Cloud, authors of *Boundaries Face to Face,* state that many people beat around the bush when having difficult conversations. The authors note several reasons for avoiding the big talk:

- You are not as direct as you want to be.
- You become argumentative instead of remaining calm and clear.
- You feel sorry for the other person and lighten up too much.
- You're too anxious.
- You break down and are overwhelmed with the pain.
- You know exactly what limits you hope to set, but you give in to more than you intended.
- You allow yourself to get sidetracked into arguments or into justifying what you think or want.
- You fear the consequences of the confrontation (rejection, disapproval, conflict) so much that the fear gets in the way of dealing with the problem.
- You have some other personal vulnerability that gets in the way.[1]

Townsend and Cloud go on to say, "You need to prepare yourself for confronting issues in a way that will make you as ready as possible and will give the interaction a better chance of being redemptive to the other person and to the relationship itself."[2]

But not so fast. We have already discussed the fact that before you can say it so he'll listen, you must first get his attention. You already have some tools that will help you do that. You must also prepare yourself. This is a basic premise of healthy relating—taking care of your own issues before you try to confront someone else about theirs.

Don't we wish it weren't so?

In the spirit of owning our issues and preparing to confront our mates, Christ said that we must first face our own problems. "Why do you look at the speck of sawdust in your brother's eye and pay no attention to the plank in your own eye? How can you say to your brother, 'Let me take the speck out of your eye,' when all the time there is a plank in your own eye?" (Matthew 7:3-4).

So, as you prepare to say it so he'll listen, stop and ask yourself whether you have dealt with your own issues. Have you looked carefully in the mirror to make sure that you are working on your issues? Are you being careful not to lay the entire burden of the problem at his feet? The conversation will be much more productive if you approach him with humility, recognizing that you are working through problems of your own.

Setting the Tone

Trish was unsettled about what to do in her relationship with Mark. He was an aspiring businessman with lofty goals, but he also said that he wanted to make room for their relationship. He acknowledged that building his business had taken a lot of his time and energy and that he had not listened to her needs. He wanted another chance. Still, Trish was uneasy. Was he simply saying he would change in order to get her back? Was he really willing to make solid changes that would enhance their relationship and prepare them for marriage? She wanted to lay out some concrete steps that would pave the way to having a serious talk with him.

Certainly, setting the tone is critical for having any serious conversation. John Gottman, author of *The Seven Principles for Making Your Marriage Work,* says, "A crucial goal of any marriage, therefore, is to create an atmosphere that encourages each person to talk honestly about his or her convictions. The more you speak candidly and respectfully with each other, the more likely there is to be a blending of your sense of meaning."[3]

On that note, Townsend and Cloud offer several practical suggestions:

First, *own your own failure to confront, and stop playing the victim.* The authors say that "to the extent that you allow someone to do something you resent, you are part of the problem." The Bible says, "Do not hate your brother in your heart. Rebuke your neighbor frankly so that you will not share his guilt" (Leviticus 19:17). If we avoid a problem, we share in the guilt of that problem.

I know that this may not be as much fun as rehearsing how we have been wronged and then nursing a grudge. However, confronting our own failures will allow us to move beyond relational conflict much sooner.

Second, *own your motives.* Be careful of "bad motives" when you approach others to settle an issue. The authors note several bad motives for approaching a friend or spouse:

- to punish or get revenge
- to make someone feel bad
- to get back at someone for things you have not dealt with
- to feel power when you have felt powerless

Here are some examples of good motives:

- to stop a bad thing from happening to you and end the hurt

- to bring to light your and the other person's contribution to a problem so you can both move forward
- to achieve greater intimacy
- to heal a breach in the relationship

Third, *own your fears.* Let's face it. Confronting someone about what they have done wrong, or even about something that you would like to see improved in your relationship, can be frightening. What if he won't talk about it? What if he listens but then indicates that he is not willing to make any changes? What if your feelings get hurt?

As you know, fear paralyzes. Fear stops us from taking a stand on important issues. Fear causes us to withdraw, downplaying the importance of our concerns. But you can face the fear and move through it, tackling the issues that are so important to you.

Fourth, *own the other person's legitimate complaints about you.* As you prepare to approach your partner with thorny issues, you must be prepared to own your part of the problem. You know that both of you have a part in the predicament and that he is likely to point out your role in it. Shrinking back from your contribution will do you no good. Face it head-on. Acknowledge that you have your own issues that you are ready to address. This by itself will make him more willing to recognize and own his part.

Jesus tells us the importance of facing our part of a problem. "Therefore, if you are offering your gift at the altar and there remember that your brother has something against you, leave your gift there in front of the altar. First go and be reconciled to your brother; then come and offer your gift" (Matthew 5:23-24).

Fifth, *own your distortions of who the other person is.* Anger and resentment have a way of clouding our perspective. In frustration, we amplify another's negative characteristics. We vilify their character. We tend to see them as all wrong and ourselves as all right. The world is much grayer than that.

Sixth, *seek understanding of the other person.* Stephen Covey emphasized this point in his book *The Seven Habits of Highly Effective People.* In this highly successful book, Covey emphasizes that we must first seek to understand others before we seek to be understood. This, of course, goes against our nature, which often demands that others understand our unique perspective.

I am reminded of one of many truths slipped between the pages of Harper Lee's Pulitzer prizewinning novel, *To Kill a Mockingbird.* Near the start of the book, Atticus, the wise father–lawyer, gives some advice to his daughter, Scout.

"First of all," he said, "if you can learn a simple trick, Scout, you'll get along a lot better with all kinds of folks. You never really understand a person until you consider things from his point of view."

"Sir?"

"—until you climb into his skin and walk around in it."[4]

Seventh, *deal with your emotions somewhere else.* Townsend and Cloud advise us to deal with our painful emotions *before* having a difficult conversation. A seeping wound and boiling anger or hurt will only serve to cloud the conversation and increase the conflict.

When two wounded people come together, a conversation rarely occurs. Each seems intent on bruising the other even more, causing an eruption that creates more wounds that need healing.

In counseling, I teach a skill called "conflict containment." Both partners temporarily set aside their anger and hurt, put it on the shelf, and then take it down at agreed-upon times. I do this for obvious reasons. If both people come to an encounter with a great deal of hurt and anger and are ready to blow up at the least provocation, healing cannot occur. Both need to set those painful feelings aside so that communication can ensue.

They often need another outlet—such as friends they can vent with—so that the air is relatively clear when they begin talking to one another.

Finally, *seek healing*. Talking to a trusted friend, pastor, or counselor will help you approach the issues objectively without becoming sidetracked into attacking the person. Bringing a balanced perspective to the bargaining table is your responsibility.[5]

These are wonderful steps to take as you begin to have conversations where you and your spouse will truly listen to each other. They offer a fantastic backdrop for saying the difficult things that must be said. They are also effective for saying the not-so-difficult things that need to be said routinely to keep the marriage fresh and vibrant.

Anatomy of a Calm Conversation

Trish prepared herself to confront Mark, first by getting his attention with the separation and then by inviting him to counseling. He agreed to attend, which was a relief to her. She was now ready to have an honest discussion with him. You too may find yourself facing a candid conversation about difficult issues. Perhaps problems have created a wall between you and your mate. What does an honest, *calm* conversation look like?

Over several weeks, I worked with Trish to help her prepare for their heart-to-heart conversation. Trish had readied herself emotionally for whatever would take place. She was focused, determined, and hopeful. She had worked through some of the steps just mentioned for having a serious conversation. She felt that her motives were healthy, and she had looked at her part of the problem. She realized that she held grudges and magnified his problems at times.

Prior to the counseling session, I felt that Trish still needed to understand the importance of conveying her message as calmly as possible. A calm word, as opposed to an angry frontal attack, creates an atmosphere where communication can truly take place. As Trish prepared for her talk, she double-checked herself for setting the tone of the conversation with these steps:

- keeping her body language open, flexible, and attentive
- speaking in "I" language, sharing her feelings and needs
- being specific, asking for exactly what she needed from Mark
- monitoring the tone of her voice, saying her words calmly
- finding ways to empathize with him, building an important rapport

After a few weeks of meeting with Trish, we invited Mark to join us. He knew the agenda was to decide if they were going to begin seeing one another again. Understandably, he was apprehensive. Yet his anxiety also served notice to him that Trish meant business.

Let's listen in on their conversation. Listen as Trish tries to speak calmly, inviting Mark into a place where he can hear her needs, feel listened to himself, and prepare to work on their relationship.

"Mark, I want you to know that I love you and would like to have our relationship work. But there are things that must change in order for me to feel comfortable in starting our relationship again."

"I know," Mark said. He looked over at me, then back at Trish.

"Well, you seem to know it now, but you didn't seem to hear me when we were seeing one another. You were preoccupied with your business and didn't seem to have time to talk about how I was feeling. I need more of your time and attention, and I especially need to have my feelings heard."

"What does that mean?" Mark said.

"I'm not sure I have communicated as clearly or calmly as I would like. It means that I want to be able to sit down and have you listen to what I say. I want you to acknowledge that you understand my feelings."

"Well, to be honest, I don't know how good I am at doing that. All I can tell you is that I'll try. I'll take more time off from work, and I'll sit down and listen to you. But you have to tell me how you're feeling."

"I can do that, Mark. I want to do that."

Fortunately, Trish and Mark were both willing to see the other in a larger perspective than just who was right or wrong. As the counseling progressed, each was able to regain sight of the person they had fallen in love with. They could see that intense conflict served only to distort their view of each other. That distortion was far removed from reality.

Trish and Mark continued to attend counseling for two months. In a relatively short time, Trish learned more about sharing her feelings honestly and calmly. She noticed that the more composed she was in dealing with Mark, the more he seemed willing and able to listen to her.

The Power of Calm Conversation

A calm voice has power. Something inside us pushes away from people who must raise their voices and become angry to get their point across. Tension distracts us from their message. When people express messages in angry, threatening tones, we raise our defenses. True sharing cannot take place.

John Gottman has studied communication in marriage. He says that he is able to predict the success or failure of a relationship based upon how the partners talk to one another in the first several minutes of a conversation.

> Statistics tell the story: 96 percent of the time you can predict the outcome of a conversation based on the first three minutes of the fifteen-minute interaction.

A harsh startup simply dooms you to failure. So if you begin a discussion that way, you might as well pull the plug, take a breather, and start over.[6]

The apostle Paul knew the power of a calm conversation. "Do not let any unwholesome talk come out of your mouths, but only what is helpful for building others up according to their needs, that it may benefit those who listen" (Ephesians 4:29). Angry outbursts and irritable tones are not the ingredients for building up others.

Gottman has some other insights worth sharing. He notes that certain types of negativity—usually occurring in an atmosphere that is anything but calm—are lethal to a relationship. He calls them the Four Horseman of the Apocalypse.

1. *Criticism:* Gottman sees a world of difference between the normal complaints that occur in a marriage—"I'm frustrated that you didn't pick up the laundry from the dry cleaners like you promised"—and criticism. Criticism is more global and attacks the person's character—"Why are you so forgetful? I'm always having to take care of things for you. It seems like you can't remember to do anything nice for me."

2. *Contempt:* Close scrutiny of how couples talk to one another reveals a painful insight: Many choose to add shame to their critical comments. Mentioning the husband has forgotten to pick up the laundry is not enough. Now she lambasts him and heaps on shame. "What is the matter with you? You don't care at all for me. I've told you twice to remember to pick up our clothes."

3. *Defensiveness:* Is it any wonder that the husband, attacked for forgetting to pick up the dry cleaning, feels defensive and retaliates? Is it any wonder that this small event becomes transformed into an inferno? In fact, minor occurrences are usually at the root of contested

encounters—all because conversations were not approached with calmness.

4. *Stonewalling:* Finally, according to Gottman, one partner has enough. He begins to tune her out. Silent treatment, distance, and avoidance dominate the relationship. The marriage grows cold, and the fabric of love is weakened, sometimes beyond repair.[7]

9/11

My son and I strolled down the cobblestone streets of Sorrento, Italy, on a warm fall afternoon several years ago. We had been out on an excursion to the island of Capri and were pleasantly tired. We walked along the street, basking in the cool Mediterranean breeze, taking in the incredible weather and scenery.

Suddenly, a large gathering of Europeans and Americans inside a café caught our attention. We glanced at the commotion and noticed that all eyes were fixed on a television mounted on the wall.

When we went inside, we saw 30 people crowded around the television, stunned into silence, watching catastrophic scenes being replayed time and again. What were we seeing? The images were horrifying—impossible, we thought. On CNN, reporters were commenting on the attack of 9/11. Like the attack on Pearl Harbor, 9/11 will forever be "a day that will live in infamy."

The Twin Towers plummeted to the ground in a molten heap. Down below, on the streets of New York, those who were not instantly killed scurried frantically to escape the carnage.

At a time of unbelievable vulnerability and fear, voices of composure and reason helped us through. In contrast to the chaos were images of the president of the United States, the governor of New York, and other officials, calmly telling Americans that we would overcome this savage attack. They repeatedly told us that we would not bow to the terrorists.

Watching this egregious act of hostility on my beloved country was difficult, especially so far away and feeling so vulnerable on foreign soil. My son and I wondered how long we might be stranded in Italy and what we would have to do to get home. No flights were leaving the country, and the State Department could only advise us to stay in a safe place for the time being. We would not know how we were going to get home for days. Our plight, of course, was miniscule compared to the experiences of those directly involved in the tremendous losses of September 11.

In all the clamor, we were thankful that our leaders and other leaders from around the globe decried the atrocities while providing reassurance that all would be well. And so it is with our relationships with one another: Calm voices are essential. Calm, genuine voices can accomplish what chaotic ones cannot. We listen to a voice that has a ring of sincerity and concern. I encourage you to practice sharing your truth with a calm, deliberate voice. See what happens.

Cloudy water, left to settle, becomes clear. Too often we attempt to make our case by attacking another person. We attempt to gain clarity and resolution through frantic activity. This rarely works. It only stirs up the water and leaves us feeling cloudier, more confused, and more baffled than when we started.

Begin now to use calmness as a powerful tool for being heard. Start by taking care of your own emotions. Find ways to settle yourself, still the inner chaos, and know what you want to communicate. Use calmness as the foundation for things that you most want to say to him.

FIVE

Saying It Clearly

I am the way, and the truth, and the life.

JOHN 14:6

⚜ ✿ ⚜

As I walk the sidewalks of Seattle, I am bombarded by disharmony: Cars honk as they jockey for position, radios boom the beat of the latest hip-hop tunes, gaudy banners draped across store windows lure customers with special offers, shoppers gaily chat about their latest finds, bus engines lend their tick-tick-tick.

As if this weren't enough for my overloaded senses, brightly dressed manikins in department store windows seem to demand that I stop in and take a look.

This is the city. For many, it is enchanting, alluring, inviting. For others, it is hectic, dissonant, chaotic. Like fingernails scraping on a blackboard. Some would rather walk barefoot on hot coals than spend a minute in the heart of Seattle.

Even those who find the city exciting are often easily satiated. Enough titillation for one day, they say. Soon it is time to retreat home to find respite from the overwhelming and disorienting sights and sounds of the metropolis.

But even in the towns surrounding the city I find narrow, busy streets lined with neon lights. Real estate signs, offerings of every form of fast food imaginable, gas stations, and quickie marts combine to create a never ending assault on the senses. Our towns never sleep.

How are we to find the rest we need? Where do we find the peaceful place that rejuvenates the soul? We know it's not available at work, but can we find it in our homes?

Walk in the front door of many homes today and you will be greeted by the blare of a television or stereo, the shouts of children, and, too often, the discord that signals conflict in a marriage. Where we look for calmness and clarity, too often we find perplexing anxiety. We turn to the medicine cabinet for help, seeking Tylenol to ease the strain or Prozac to help lift the terrible load we carry. We are desperate for something that can provide relief.

One stressful day leads to another. Soon, we are moving through life in a daze, expecting to be bombarded with extraneous stimulation. Often we do not even know how confused we are. We are unaware of how jumbled our lives have become until we have something to contrast them with.

Recently, I spent a weekend at a cabin on Hood Canal, enjoying a panoramic view of the Olympic Mountains. In the solitude of time set apart to write and reflect, absent the usual interruptions of phone, television, newspapers, and radio, I was able to see things clearly. Standing outside, I was mesmerized by the rugged Olympics, nudging one another to reach even higher into the crystal sky. Snowcapped peaks stood as a backdrop to the deep, blue waters of Hood Canal. Everything was in sharp focus. The mountains rose in sharp relief against the sky, and the water nestled against the edge of dark green forests. Crisp lines marked where one element ended and another began.

Inside, I was blessed with equal clarity. In the silence, I reached a better understanding about why certain things had been troubling me. I reflected on new directions I wanted to take. I considered things that I needed to say to important people in my life.

A hodgepodge of issues began to untangle and take on distinction. I rehearsed how I might take action, how I might speak to things that had been confusing to me only days earlier. Sometimes, we just need quiet time in a tranquil place to find ourselves.

Helen Keller

I *chose* to spend a brief period of time in a silent, restful retreat, free from the usual blur of daily life, but Helen Keller had no choice. Her world was void of sight and sound for nearly all of her 87 years. Having lost her ability to hear or see at the age of 19 months, she could not remember ever having seen a sunset, having heard the buzz of a crowd, or having endured bitter words spoken to harm. Her external world was calm, but her inner world was filled with turmoil.

While her sensory world was eerily quiet, Helen Keller still had to contend with acrimony. She had to struggle with parents who did not like one another and lived in a marriage without love and affection. Because of her affliction,

> no one had the heart to discipline her. She was willful and quick-tempered by nature and tyrannized the household. She smashed dishes and lamps, plunged her hands into people's plates.... Helen could neither see nor hear other people's reactions and had no idea of the pain she inflicted. Her parents' tears and recriminations had no impact on her.[1]

In spite of this horrific beginning, Helen Keller's name eventually became synonymous with the indomitable spirit of one who overcame incredible obstacles to live a productive, even illustrious, life. Through the help of Annie Sullivan, whom she referred to as "Teacher," Helen became a crusader for the blind. Out of her inner chaos she found spiritual and emotional clarity. She went on to inspire thousands.

Perhaps what is so amazing about Helen Keller is that she could so easily have turned out to be a person who floundered. She could have wallowed in anger and self-pity. She could have continued to emulate the unhappiness she sensed between her parents. Instead, she learned to see things clearly, understand things clearly, say things clearly. She is someone we can look to as a model for how to find significance and meaning in a fractured world.

Ruth

Many characters in the Bible seem to have the inner strength and clarity we see in Helen Keller. Ruth is one of the best examples.

The story of Ruth begins with the unfortunate circumstances of another woman, Naomi. She was widowed in a strange land, enough of a disability for anyone. Although she had two sons whom she undoubtedly counted on to see her through, they both died. She was alone in a hostile land, without the protection of a husband or sons. She had only her two daughters-in-law to rely on.

In a magnanimous decision, Naomi chooses to send them back to their home country, where they will have some chance of finding husbands again. But Ruth will not leave her mother-in-law; where Naomi goes, Ruth is determined to go as well. She places her own future aside out of love and loyalty to Naomi.

What Naomi initially shares with Helen Keller, besides a devastating turn of events that channeled her life, is hopelessness. What Helen shares with Naomi is the feeling that "the LORD's hand has gone out against me." Perhaps this book finds you in similar despair. Perhaps you have tried to salvage what is left of a situation, only to have the wind knocked out of your sails.

In the midst of this poignant biblical story, Ruth sends her message to Naomi calmly and clearly.

Don't urge me to leave you or to turn back from you.
Where you go I will go, and where you stay I will stay.
Your people will be my people and your God my
God. Where you die I will die, and there I will be
buried. May the LORD deal with me, be it ever so se-
verely, if anything but death separates you and me
(Ruth 1:16-17).

I want to call your attention to the next verses, for they are
critical to our understanding of the message of this chapter: We
often need to say what needs to be said as clearly as possible,
without extra words that only serve to raise the defenses of the
other person or confuse the situation. What was Naomi's response?

"When Naomi realized that Ruth was determined to go
with her, she stopped urging her. So the two women went on
until they came to Bethlehem" (1:18-19).

Done deal. The issue was settled. A transaction had been
completed. Naomi would not beg Ruth to go back to her own
country. The two women would no longer cry for what had happened to them; that was in the past. They would not bemoan
their condition; that time had expired. They would press on together.

Sixty-seven words. It must have taken Ruth all of a minute
to say what she needed to say, maybe less. Naomi offered no rebuttal. Ruth knew what was important to her; she understood
the most salient points of her message. She presented her case
in sharp, clear language. This was not a debate. It was a statement of how Ruth chose to run her life. It was so succinct and
incisive that Naomi had little choice but to concede. Naomi
could see the wisdom of the position and said, in essence, "All
right, let's go."

As was the case with Helen Keller and Annie Sullivan, a
friendship had been forged. Ruth and Naomi's union of gritty
determination was focused on a sole objective—getting through

this together. Helen's union with her mentor, friend, and teacher, Annie Sullivan, was sometimes threatened. Here too a clearly stated message was enough to solidify the relationship. Helen reportedly said, "If I have to decide between my mother and Teacher, I will stay with Teacher."[2]

Ruth understood the art of communication. She recognized, perhaps partly through the counsel of her wise mother-in-law, the times to speak and the times to be silent. She learned the art of clarity in her communication, and ultimately, this provided her prosperity. She followed Naomi's clear, convincing counsel, and this provided direction for their lives. She was saved from her desperate circumstances into the safety of a loving and protective husband. Naomi found shelter under the umbrella of Ruth's protection as well.

The Lens of the Biochemist

Both of my sons, Joshua, now a medical student, and Tyson, who now works for Habitat for Humanity while considering his life direction, were biochemists. This is a world quite foreign to me. In the laboratory, they worked tirelessly, adding and subtracting elements, working to find cures for diseases. They began with many different theories and substances. Gradually, they narrowed the elements to a few so that they could understand which element was having which effect on the others. The final task, however, was to distill the substances to find the purest compound. They were scientists, seeking the unadulterated truth. They sought clarity, using the filters of the laboratory and rigid scientific protocol.

The prophet Isaiah sought similar clarity and truth. He spoke clearly during difficult times for Israel. When rebellion was rampant in the land, Isaiah had some harsh things to say. He often used the imagery of the refiner's fire to illustrate the importance of seeking purity.

Isaiah chastened Israel. "Your silver has become dross, your choice wine is diluted with water" (Isaiah 1:22). He prophesies, "I will thoroughly purge away your dross and remove your impurities" (1:25).

The Lord wanted purity among His people. He wanted the impurities to be filtered away; He wanted His children to listen to His voice and respond. His words remain applicable to today, especially to our message of speaking with clarity. He said of the Israelites:

> Be ever hearing, but never understanding;
> be ever seeing, but never perceiving.
> Make the heart of this people calloused;
> make their ears dull
> and close their eyes.
> Otherwise they might see with their eyes,
> hear with their ears,
> understand with their hearts,
> and turn and be healed (6:9-10).

The people of Israel were calloused. They possessed ears that could not seem to hear, eyes that could not seem to see. But the Lord offered a way to see, to hear, to understand, and to be healed.

I think the same situation exists today. We have the opportunity to be in relationships where other people are able to hear us, see us, and understand what we are saying. The result? Turning away from the distractions and being healed.

Say What You Mean

Frequently, I find myself asked to be a referee in marital disputes. I listen to couples who erroneously think that if one bowls the other over with enough words, someone will emerge as the winner. They seem to believe that whoever can confuse his or her partner will be victorious.

Perhaps you have tried to use the perceived power of a multitude of words to change another's mind. In actuality, a flurry of words will not win an argument. In fact, it will only serve to annoy the listener. Few things are more frustrating than trying to have a discussion with someone but becoming lost in his or her murky arguments.

Perhaps you have been guilty of confounding the situation by rambling on, never getting to the point. This is an easy trap to fall into. Unsure of exactly what we want to say, we use a lot of words and hope the message comes through in one way or another. But that seldom happens.

Helen and Rich came to see me after reaching an impasse in their marriage. They told me they had been married for 30 years and wanted to save their relationship. Neither expressed any desire to get out.

Helen was a large woman, dressed immaculately, who carried herself with an air of distinction. Nails polished bright red, every hair in place, she spoke firmly and directly. She worked as an office manager for a local dentist.

Rich was an equally refined, slightly graying man. He was as verbally skilled as his wife.

As we began our session, I asked them to tell me why they had come in for counseling. At first, both deferred to the other. Here was a polite and dignified couple, I surmised.

After some initial pleasantries, the truth emerged. Helen set the stage. Her words flowed slowly at first but soon picked up steam.

She began by telling me that Rich was critical of her having a glass of wine every evening. She described his habit of telling her how annoyed he was at her for drinking, how badly he made her feel, and how he used shame to try to get her to quit. She explained that she had started to hide her drinking but resented having to do so because she really didn't think one glass of wine was excessive.

Rich waited patiently for her to stop talking. When she indicated that she was finished, he took up his cause. He admitted that he hated her drinking; his father had been an alcoholic, and Rich had suffered through years of abuse as a child. He listed the problems associated with alcohol use and told me how embarrassed he felt about her drinking. He continued talking for more than ten minutes.

Rich finally turned to me.

"So, you can see why we need your help. We go through this every day but don't seem to get anywhere. She is intent on drinking and hiding her booze, and I can't trust her anymore."

Then Helen added her rebuttal.

"And you can see why I have to hide my drinking. He is critical of every little thing I do, and I can't get him to leave me alone."

I looked at Helen and Rich. Such a nice-looking couple, with so much going for them. Married 30 years with three grown children, they were now watching their golden years evaporate. They had so many verbal skills and did so much sharing, but they made so little progress. Theirs was a classic case of too many words and too little clarity. Each used much effort to persuade the other of the error of his or her ways, but they used so little effort to find ways of living peacefully with one another.

It was another version of Blame the Other for My Problem.

"If she would just quit drinking, I'd be happy."

"If he would just quit scolding me for having a glass of wine, I'd be happy."

I suspect you could insert your names into the story. Most of us have, at one time or another, gotten into a power struggle with our partner over some issue. In the process, we lose sight of the big picture and focus on changing the other person. We blame him or her for our problem and use the one weapon we have at our disposal: words. Befuddling words. Confounding words. Vilifying words. Emotionally laden words.

When you stand back and look at an encounter like Helen and Rich's, you can see how silly their words are. Rich is silly to try to talk Helen out of drinking a glass of wine. His true concern is obscured by emotion and a lack of directness. For example, you never hear him simply say how he feels when she drinks.

The truth is, a case can be made for the foolishness of both parties. We could just as easily defend him as her. Both arguments have some validity. But we could just as easily challenge both parties. Both are using ineffective techniques to address the problem.

Confusing Words Create a Battlefield

What could be wrong with using a few extra words?

First, *using excessive words often signals that we are trying to manipulate our partner.* We use words to judge other people. When we say too many words, the message usually carries judgment, shame, anger, and intimidation.

If you have had the unique pleasure of raising an adolescent, you know what I am talking about. Watch any adolescent trying to extend his or her curfew for the upcoming dance, and you will witness communication skills that could rival those of any Wall Street attorney. The words come at you from the left, then the right, all part of a full-scale, over-the-top attack.

Finally, in frustration, utterly exhausted, you scream, "What part of 'no' don't you understand?"

Second, *a confusing message creates frustration in the listener.* It leaves the listener wondering what is happening. They may be giving you their full attention, but their brain is saying, *I can't figure out what this person is trying to tell me. She keeps talking, but I can't make heads or tails of it.*

You will know you are losing your mate during a discussion if...

- His eyes glaze over.
- He interrupts you.

- He leaves angrily.
- He keeps asking you to get to your point.

Third, *a message without clarity and focus drains a relationship.* A confusing conversation is nothing more than a bunch of words, passed back and forth without purpose. At some level, both partners know the conversation is going nowhere, and if they have been through this many times before, they know it will end in futility.

Fourth, *a confusing message shows a lack of respect for the other person.* Talking without clarity indicates a failure to take the other person seriously. It is a way of saying, "I want to talk and talk and hear myself talk, but I don't really want to make the effort to speak so that you will understand me."

Finally, *confusing language is often a way of taking yourself too seriously.* Yes, when we talk and talk and refuse to get to the heart of our message, we are usually taking ourselves far too seriously. We think that our perspective is the only valid point of view. This perspective is, of course, very detrimental to the relationship.

I recently worked with a couple who engaged in conversation that violated nearly every principle we talk about in this book. Sadly, many of us are guilty of the same thing.

Frank and Bethany had been married for more than ten years when they came in for counseling. Frank was a recovering alcoholic, and the years of drinking had left him with a tough outer and inner edge. His rough, pale skin showed the lines of too many late nights. He was still quite temperamental, and this created some distance between him and his wife. She longed for greater intimacy.

Bethany had endured these challenging years and, with a toughness of her own, tended, in Frank's words, to "nip at my heels." She was grateful that he had quit drinking, but she wanted the closeness she had lived without for years. She did not know how to ask for it.

Bethany had a number of concerns, even with Frank's new sobriety. She wanted communication, whereas there had been years of distance. She wanted them to get out and have some fun, whereas for years she had been home alone with the kids. She wanted them to be financially solvent, whereas for years she had lived with the uncertainty of unpaid bills and credit card debt. She wanted a lot, and Frank felt the weight of her demands.

But her demands were not what brought them in for counseling. It was her demeanor. Her abrasive, abrupt, demanding style was cloaked in a rambling manner that confused and angered Frank.

"I don't know what you are trying to tell me," he would say. "You keep nipping at me and won't leave me alone."

Hurt and angry herself, Bethany vacillated between retreating and challenging him even more forcefully. When neither of those approaches worked, she pouted and let him know that he had wounded her. Sometimes he felt badly about this; often he simply let her sulk.

Fortunately, Bethany was willing to practice healthier communication skills. She was willing to practice saying things calmly and clearly. This did not come naturally or easily to her, but she was excited to have these new skills. And Frank appreciated them as well. He was willing to hear her and attempt to meet her needs. Things between them improved dramatically in a short period of time.

Your task is to bring clarity to your words. You can do this by...

- clearly saying what you mean and meaning what you say
- clearly speaking with simple and direct words
- clearly asking for what you need
- clearly owning your part of the problem
- clearly making a resolution of accountability for change

Armed with new tools, Bethany changed how she approached Frank.

"Frank," she said. "I still want you to date me, even though we are no longer newlyweds. I want to feel special to you."

"I can do that," he answered.

"And I want you to remind me if I start nagging. I will work on saying what I need in a clearer voice instead of nagging at you."

"That would help a bunch."

"And I am tired of having too many bills. Can we sit down together to get our finances straight?"

"Well, we have a lot of bills. And we have a lot of work ahead of us. But sure, let's figure it out together."

Frank and Bethany's talk may sound unusually easy, but clear communication often dissipates tension.

Truth That Heals

Talking about the importance of clarity is impossible without mentioning truth. Clarity without truth is not clarity. A vision of something without truth is a blind alley. It is as helpful as an outdated map.

Truth can be painful, but it is healing. The Bible says that you can know the truth, and the truth will set you free. Consider how that works. How can the truth provide clarity and freedom? Let me offer an example.

A 45-year-old man named Jason comes to see me for long-standing symptoms of depression. He is tired, unhappy, easily irritated, and sleeps poorly. Before we can make much progress, I must make a diagnosis. Is this man's problem really depression? Perhaps it is a temporary grief reaction stemming from recent losses, and the only thing to do is wait out the long hours of sadness that will lead to recovery.

Perhaps his malaise stems from his medical condition, a series of autoimmune difficulties that have left him weak and listless. Medications and rest may be all that is needed.

Perhaps his condition is situational, owing to his recent financial setbacks. He may be discouraged over losses he has taken in the stock market, and a visit to his financial planner may be more useful than a visit to a shrink.

Could he be frustrated by working rotating shifts at the plywood mill where he is employed? And what about his marriage? Could some of his sadness stem from distance he feels between himself and his wife, Wendy? Could pent-up frustration and anger be taking a toll on his emotional health?

During our inquiry, the most prominent theme for Jason was "I shouldn't be depressed." As you might guess, this is not a helpful approach. If, each time we consider a possible cause for his exhaustion and unhappiness, he says, "That shouldn't make me depressed," our attempts to help him come to a screeching halt. Our first task must be helping him take off his judgmental blindfold so that he can see things clearly.

As we talk, we ferret out the wheat from the chaff. I determine that he has clinical depression and that his course of treatment should include medications as well as psychotherapy. He has become passive about the lack of positive activities in his life, and he has become bored and depressed about his mundane existence. We decide, together, that he needs to take an active interest in finding his spiritual calling and living out his spiritual gifts, as well as finding joy in life again. In short, we have gone on a search for truth and clarity, knowing that it will set him free.

Part of Jason's issues, as you might expect, included speaking clearly to his wife about ways to improve their relationship. He has been reluctant to talk to her candidly, fearing that he would hurt her feelings. But, we agreed, keeping his unhappiness to himself would not help their relationship or his depression. Speaking truthfully and sensitively to her helped to heal both

Jason and his marriage. He was able to tell her some things that had been missing for him in their marriage, and he was surprised to find that she had wanted some of the same changes.

The Power of Clear Communication

In her bestselling book *Loving What Is,* Byron Katie has prompted many to explore more deeply what is true for them and then speak the truth to both themselves and others. Katie has taken some obvious, simple statements—such as telling yourself the truth—and demonstrated ways to make them practical.

According to Katie, much of our suffering stems from our unwillingness to see or speak truthfully. She says, "The truth is whatever is in front of you, whatever is really happening. Whether you like it or not, it's raining now. 'It shouldn't be raining' is just a thought....These are only thoughts we impose on reality."[3]

In my opinion, Katie is right. We too often dwell on what we wish others had done for us. We dwell on how we think others ought to live. We wish they would read our minds and magically meet our every need. We tell ourselves, *I shouldn't have to tell him what I want.*

Once we have bravely faced reality—specifically, the way things are and not simply how we'd like them to be—and owned it, we are then in a position to talk about it with our mate. Facing a problem and owning it, without all the baggage of "shoulds" and "oughts," empowers us because we are preparing to share the truth with another and make changes that will set us free.

This can be scary business. Facing the truth and living out the power of clear communication is frightening. But if we are willing to look in the mirror and are utterly truthful with ourselves about our problems, we stand ready to take the next step: action. We are ready, feeble knees and all, to stand with our spouse and clearly speak the truth. Not what is true for them— that is their business. Rather, what is true for us.

The following action steps represent a starting point:

- Tell yourself the truth about your life.
- Think about what this truth means to your relationships.
- Talk to your spouse about what is true for you.

Let me warn you, however: Clear communication has the power to set things into motion. Clear communication sets boundaries in our love lives. Clear communication alerts others to who we are and what is important to us. Clear communication sets us up to have others tell us yes and no. Ultimately, it creates the groundwork for a real, honest relationship. It is very rewarding, but it can also be very risky. In the long run, it is worthwhile.

By now you have learned the importance of getting your man's attention. You know the importance of saying things calmly and clearly. Let's now focus on saying things concisely.

Six

Saying It Concisely

Simplify, simplify, simplify.

HENRY DAVID THOREAU

Recently, my friend Rob, a portly New York transplant who is known for getting straight to the point, invited me to a Toastmasters meeting. I had always likened Toastmasters to other mysterious groups such as the Elks, Moose, and Rainbow, but Rob assured me that it would be a lot of fun. Besides, he said, I would learn how to be a more effective speaker in the process.

I was dubious. I have been a psychologist for many years and make a living talking to people. They generally like me, I like them, and my ability to communicate seems quite effective. I have traveled widely, promoting my books and giving countless radio and television interviews. What could this group possibly teach me?

For months I dragged my feet while my friend chided me to join. But my resolve not to participate evaporated quite suddenly after a phone conversation with my publicist. After reviewing a recent television appearance, she suggested that I needed to improve my speaking abilities.

I took the news like most males: I wanted to scream at her through the phone. I managed to contain my irritation and embarrassment and asked for feedback. (Never do this unless you are solidly prepared for the response.)

To my astonishment, she told me that I needed to get to the point more quickly. She told me that what I had to say was interesting but that I tended to ramble. She had the audacity to compare my presentations to rabbit trails. I wanted to believe that she had me confused with some other loquacious author, but I knew that she had me pegged.

Unsure of my message, I thought that I could hide behind an overabundance of words. Like a middle school student who believes that more pages will earn a better grade, I thought that more words meant more meaning. I had forgotten a simple rule: Say it concisely. Give folks a couple of ideas to chew on and leave them wanting more. This sounded simple enough. Perhaps it was time to give Toastmasters a try. I would show up, dazzle them with my oratory abilities, win some well-deserved acclaim, and leave them wanting more.

After a safe, introductory meeting at Toastmasters, I signed up for my first speech. *This shouldn't be hard,* I kept telling myself. They had even provided guidelines: Keep the speech to two minutes and avoid the infamous "um." How tough could that be?

I began preparing my speech, "Ways to Relate to Your Teen." The initial preparation was not difficult. The words flowed. And flowed. And flowed. I had so much I wanted to say about teenagers and about how to establish an effective relationship with them.

But after writing the speech, I realized that coming in under the prescribed time limit would be no easy matter. How could I pare down a thirty-minute dissertation to two minutes?

Without a doubt, Toastmasters has proven more rigorous than I had imagined. Producing concise, clear communication is not merely an art. It is a skill that must be practiced.

Men and Words

I readily admit that I am more talkative than most men. I have a gift of gab that many men lack. Though somewhat skilled with words, my listening abilities need work, especially in my personal life. More than once my sons have encouraged me to listen more carefully to what they say. I may have two ears, but after about three minutes of conversation only one of them seems to work. Like most men, I want the speaker to get to the heart of the matter as quickly as possible.

Let's not waste time wondering why men's attention spans are so short and their speaking abilities so limited. Instead, let's spend our time understanding how to work with men's limitations so that you can get your message across to your man. After all, that is what you want.

You remember Frank and Bethany from our last chapter. Bethany was frustrated with her marriage because she could not communicate effectively with Frank. He protested that Bethany nipped at his heels. This is not an unusual complaint. Men often feel that women are trying to control them, prying into their inner lives, pushing relentlessly for more information. How does this nagging bombardment of words make men feel?

- attacked
- belittled
- insecure
- frightened
- angry
- defensive

In response, many retreat in despair. As I found out from my publicist, an abundance of words simply loses the audience. Similarly, when men are bombarded with a mountain of words—especially words with an edge—they turn off. They retreat. They clam up.

David Clarke offers the following advice:

Ladies, let me guess. You start 98% of the conversations with your husbands, don't you? You talk about your day. You describe the events in your life. You share your emotions. If he doesn't react to what you share, you ask him questions.

How is this approach working? Is your man responding by talking about his own life and sharing his emotions? I doubt it. When you begin virtually all the conversations, you are being a crowbar....Not only do you start too many conversations, you also carry too many conversations. How can I say this delicately, with sensitivity? You talk too much. You fill the air with words and overwhelm the man's weak listening apparatus. He tunes you out, you catch him, and you're angry and hurt. The conversation is over. And if he doesn't tune you out, and is actually listening, it won't make any difference. The more words you use, the higher his resistance to talking. He can't compete with your impressive verbiage, so he won't even try. Plus, he can't get a word in edgewise in the face of the avalanche of sentences.[1]

Dr. Clarke is very confrontational. But he makes his point clearly. We have a choice. We can sit back and squirm, believing that Clarke is out of line and that he has greatly exaggerated the problem. But perhaps a better option is to listen to what he has to say and consider the possibility that his observations are accurate. Could it be that most women have more words available to them than men do? That women are inclined to keep talking beyond a man's comfort level? That women have a tougher time saying what they want to say in a concise manner? That women add to a man's innate defensiveness by going on and on when fewer words would be more effective? Could Clarke possibly be right?

Bethany took partial responsibility for creating an atmosphere where Frank felt nipped at. When she sat back and looked critically at her behavior, she could see where she had let frustration influence her message. She let too much emotion and too many words obscure her meaning. After spending a good deal of time in counseling, Bethany decided to try making her point to Frank in a more direct, concise manner.

Let's review again what worked more effectively for her. After much consideration and preparation on her part, which helped her develop inner clarity, she asked Frank for specific things:

- Frank's attention as she prepared him for a heart-to-heart conversation
- more dates that involved special time to enjoy one another
- his assistance in correcting their financial problems
- a reminder if she slipped back into nagging

She gave Frank some things in return:

- her calm, clear attention
- her willingness to talk in a way that he is more likely to listen to
- her commitment to change her part of the communication problem

Needless to say, Bethany's new approach had a more favorable reaction from Frank. No miracles occurred, but Frank was far less defensive and more receptive when Bethany used the tools she learned.

A Lot of Work

At this point, some of you may be saying, "This is too much work! Is the art of communication really this difficult? Must I really learn all of these new skills?"

Yes and yes.

Learning to communicate effectively really is work. The challenges that accompany being in a relationship never cease to amaze me. Even the most enduring marriages are not immune to the ravages of poor communication. I routinely see 20-, 30-, and even 40-year marriages disintegrate, primarily because the partners have failed to keep the lines of communication open.

Communicating with friends or lovers in the early stages of a relationship may be fun and relatively pain free. But after a while, the work that accompanies keeping things alive must begin. Even seasoned, effective communicators must remind themselves to keep an open mind, to share their message calmly and clearly, and to listen intently to their partner.

And yes, you must learn these skills. There is simply no way around it. Refuse to learn these skills at your peril. If you decide that you will coast by with the skills you already have, be prepared for the relationship to falter somewhere down the road. Don't be surprised if your spouse becomes dissatisfied and feels neglected, abused, or mistreated. Prepare for difficulties to arise.

Remember the reason we are practicing these skills: You want to get your message to your man. You want him to really listen to you and to respond appropriately. You want him to take you seriously. You want him to really hear you. You want him to listen with his heart as well as his ears.

If he does that, he will have your best interests in mind and be more likely to go out of his way to create the loving relationship you so desire.

The Wedding at Cana

The apostle John writes that this was Jesus' first sign.

Jesus and His disciples are invited to a wedding celebration. When the wine is gone, Jesus' mother comes to Him, complaining about the situation.

"They have no more wine," she says.

"Why do you involve me?" He says, but He actually seems to be asking, "What is your point?" He might have wondered why she would bring this problem to Him, as if He were the sommelier of the ceremony.

She says nothing more to Him but turns to the servants and says, "Do whatever He tells you." If you or I were put in that situation, I suspect we would have snapped at our mother and then offered a lecture to both her and the servants. Instead, Jesus concisely says what He wants. His message is clear and to the point.

"Fill the jars with water." So they filled them to the brim.

Then He told them, "Now draw some out and take it to the master of the banquet" (John 2:7-8).

These simple and incisive instructions were enough to get the job done. Jesus could have explained to the servants what He was doing, but He does not feel that is necessary. He could have taken more elaborate steps to replenish the wine, but He chooses to act quietly and with no wasted motion.

The water, as we know, miraculously changes to wine and receives rave reviews. The master of the banquet is astounded and compliments the bridegroom for saving the best wine for last.

A reading of the Gospels provides us with many concise messages from Jesus. He was certainly capable of expounding on a subject, but He often used words sparingly and for special purposes. He dealt with many situations quickly and concisely:

- inviting His disciples to come with Him
- weaving together parables to give a message
- responding to the criticisms of the religious leaders
- scolding the Pharisees for their self-righteousness
- encouraging followers to believe in Him
- challenging His disciples to understand His message
- explaining His relationship to His Father

The garden scene, before Jesus' death, provides an example of His clear, concise speaking. He said to His disciples, "Sit here while I pray" (Mark 14:32). He then says to Peter, James, and John, "My soul is overwhelmed with sorrow to the point of death....Stay here and keep watch" (14:34). A few moments later, He pleads with the Father: "Abba, Father...everything is possible for you. Take this cup from me. Yet not what I will, but what you will" (14:36).

No one would dispute the fact that Jesus was an eloquent speaker. We see glimpses of His skills in the Sermon on the Mount and His many parables. He was capable of keeping crowds spellbound. People commonly sat at His feet for hours just to listen to Him. Undoubtedly, He spoke with passion, delivering a message that met a deep need for His audience.

Sometimes He spoke at length, but at other times He spoke only briefly.

In many ways, Jesus' message can be summarized in one verse:

"For God so loved the world that he gave his one and only Son, that whoever believes in him shall not perish but have eternal life" (John 3:16).

Many have tried to make the message more complicated. This is not necessary.

Many have tried to circumvent the message. This cannot be done.

Many have tried to ignore the message. This is not possible.

Sharon and Jack

Sharon and Jack have been married for eight years. Both are in their early thirties. They have two young sons. They came for counseling at Sharon's insistence because she was frustrated by their lack of communication. She felt that Jack did not listen to her or attempt to meet her needs.

Sharon is a thin, lively, professional woman who works as a marketing specialist for a local hospital. Because of her job, she has to travel several days each month and must also attend evening meetings. Jack is a slender, muscular, soft-spoken man who looks at home in jeans and a T-shirt. He works as a laboratory technician at the same hospital.

The air was charged as they looked at one another with obvious frustration. I took down a brief history of their marriage. In the early stages of their relationship, they had plenty of time for communication. Actually, they told me they had no problem communicating at all when they first met. The relationship was new and exciting and had enough sparks to light a fire. Even when Sharon had to travel, they found a way to talk every day, often for hours.

After they were married, things began to change. Let's listen to Sharon tell her story.

"I am so frustrated," Sharon said, as Jack looked on dispassionately. "And I am so angry. I want him to talk to me, but I can't get two words out of him. I want him to share something deeper than just how his work is going. I want a relationship with him, but that never seems to happen. He especially seems to resent my travel, but he knew that was part of my job when we got married. When I'm gone, he needs to pick up the slack by getting the kids off to school and picking them up. But that seems to be too much for him. He also needs to help keep the house clean. But I come home to a mess after traveling, and that exhausts me."

"So what happens when you try to talk to one another?" I asked.

At that point, Jack jumped in.

"She's always upset with me. That's all I ever hear. All the stuff I'm doing wrong. A guy gets tired of it."

"Yes, I am upset," Sharon said. "Who wouldn't be? We're supposed to have a marriage, not a mother-son relationship.

Why do I have to pick up all the pieces? Why do I have to start every conversation? Why is everything up to me?"

Jack didn't respond. He simply looked at Sharon, then back at me.

Jack and Sharon obviously had a number of issues that were forming a barrier between them. And the *way* they communicated—or failed to communicate, in this instance—was clearly causing huge problems.

As I listened to Sharon vent, I wondered how she dealt with all that hostility. I also wondered what Jack must feel like when Sharon continually dumped her complaints on him. Both were clearly hurting; both needed relief.

Every book on marital communication notes the importance of *meaningful communication*—the ability to be heard and understood by another person. Simply talking to one another is not enough. Words alone do not create communication.

It is impossible. Jack and Sharon cannot possibly communicate meaningfully. They are experiencing too much tension at this point. As you listen to Sharon, you can see that her message gets lost along the way. One of the reasons it gets lost is that she has trouble getting her point across concisely. She jumps from one issue to another with far too much emotion for Jack.

Barriers to Concise Communication

We might agree that concise communication is laudable, but we must admit that it is also hard to achieve. As we listen to Sharon, we can certainly empathize with her difficulties. We can feel her pain. We want Jack to carry his load. We want him to help around the house so Sharon can return to a neat and orderly home. We want her to be able to share her feelings with Jack and for them to enjoy intimacy again.

But we can also empathize with Jack. We want him to be appreciated for the things he *is* doing right. We can understand his anger at being criticized continuously. We know the feeling of being nagged and humiliated. Neither Jack nor Sharon feels appreciated. For that reason, they are unwilling to be vulnerable with each other.

Consider some of the issues that might derail you from speaking concisely to your man. Did you see some of these issues in Sharon's relationship with Jack?

First, *words come easily to you.* For most women, using self-restraint when you talk is a hefty challenge. Words bombard the brain, and many women may feel compelled to share them.

I have watched countless women unwittingly overwhelm their men. I don't think they wanted to overwhelm them, at least not in most instances. Women simply have an abundance of words, and they feel a need to share them. This is especially true when they are under stress.

Second, *you have so much you want to say.* You have a lot that you want to get off your mind (and onto his). At times, your thoughts are like water building behind a dam. When the dam opens, words spill out.

The water can spill out, but it needs to come through the spillway. You create a spillway by taking one issue at a time, measuring your words, and watching his reaction so that you don't overwhelm him.

Third, *you have so much passion about what you want to say.* Measuring your words is difficult when so much emotion is attached to them. When we care about something deeply, we must work to detach ourselves from our words. But that is what we must do.

Emotion has been called energy in motion (e-motion). Strong feelings almost always demand expression. Perhaps you were at home one evening, looking at your spouse and experiencing a wellspring of emotions. You began to add up all of his infractions. You hadn't prepared for a talk, you didn't bother to ask if that was a good time to have a discussion, and you didn't measure your words. You simply set the energy in motion and allowed the words to follow.

The e-motion takes over. You tell him how selfish he is, how demanding, how uncaring. Every complaint you have bottled up pours out. And then, surprise! He becomes defensive.

Of course, you attack him for becoming defensive. Why can't he take the heat? He is the one who committed the offenses. He is the one who hurt you. He deserves this.

Later, after you have calmed down, you may feel some embarrassment because of your actions. Yet, to prevent feeling badly, you rationalize your behavior. After all, you tell yourself, you didn't say anything that was not the truth.

But this "truth" cut like a knife. It violated every rule we are learning about healthy communication. Your strategy simply did not work. It did not bring you closer to your desired end—to be listened to, to be understood, and to experience real change.

Unbridled emotion almost always creates havoc. Like the water behind the dam, emotions are ready to move. Like the spark in the forest, emotions are capable of creating a great blaze. If the spark is not controlled, a lot of damage can occur.

Fourth, *you have never considered that you should limit your words.* For some readers, the thought of managing their words by being concise and calm has never occurred to them. Perhaps this applies to you. Perhaps you have thought that you should be able to say whatever you want.

Saying things concisely requires discipline. Yes, I know— many of us dislike that word. It implies work. Deep within each of us is a voice that wants to say whatever it feels like saying. This voice does not want to be restricted. It does not want to be bothered with preparation or kindness or responsibility.

But each of us must face the fact that lectures don't work. They never have. They didn't work when our parents gave them to us, and they don't work when we give them to our partners.

Finally, *many words often lead to many demands.* When we shift into "lecture mode," we usually also shift into "demand mode." We move away from thoughtful communication to something else. I am not exactly sure what it is, but it is definitely not communication.

Willard Harley, in his book *Love Busters,* notes that unbridled words often lead to making demands of your spouse—demands that frequently create resentment.

> Demands are a shortsighted way to force people to meet our needs. Knowing that people will not enjoy doing what we want, we insist they do it anyway. If they comply, they won't like it and, as a result, will never be in the habit of helping us....But demands are also thoughtless. Our gains come at the expense of others: We don't care how they feel as long as we get our way. For that reason, when we make demands of our spouses, we withdraw love units, robbing marriage of romantic love.[2]

Sharon and Jack needed to learn some new skills. Sharon's old habits were not working for her or for her marriage. Fortunately, she was willing to practice some new techniques that drastically altered Jack's willingness to listen to her and attempt to meet her needs.

Our first task was to limit the number of issues on the table. We could not address every problem in one fell swoop, much to Sharon's dismay. She was used to multitasking and wanted to handle her marriage like a business transaction. "Let's just do it all and get it over with" seemed to be her motto. Obviously, that approach was not working in her marriage.

Once she had agreed to deal with one issue at a time, Sharon began working on taking some of the emotion out of her message. Jack was able to listen to her much more easily when she spoke calmly, clearly, and concisely. She told him how important it was for her to come home to a clean house. He began to understand that and was willing to work on it. Sharon also began limiting her words. She finally admitted that lectures don't work.

Together, Jack and Sharon slowly rebuilt their marriage, one communication lesson at a time. Together, each of them learned to send messages in ways the other was more likely to hear. By utilizing these skills and eliminating barriers to saying things concisely, they achieved real progress.

Some Final Tools

You may be wondering if you will be able to say what you want to say in a concise manner. Will speaking concisely take the lifeblood out of your message? No. With practice you will be able to say all that is important, with the passion you feel, in a way he will be able to hear. As you move toward expressing yourself succinctly, several additional tools can be helpful to you. These are tools that you already know; you simply need to recall them and practice them.

- *Consider what you want to say.* As you read this book, you are undoubtedly reminded of things that you want to get across to your man. That is the heart of this book—saying it so he'll listen. But what is it, exactly, that you want to say? What is the heart of the message?

- *Clear preparation.* You will have much greater success in getting your message to him if you prepare. What is the best time to talk to him? What is the best location? The best setting? You want him to be as comfortable as possible when you say what needs to be said. Preparation can yield great dividends.

- *Rehearse your message.* A discussion of heated issues often goes better after you have rehearsed in your mind, or with a friend, exactly what you want to say. Consider the heart of your message and how you might say it more succinctly.

- *Know when to stop.* This may be the most difficult goal to accomplish. Know when you have made your point and stop talking. Sooner rather than later is often best. Know when to say when.

You are beginning to learn a number of useful skills that will advance you toward your goal of getting your message to your man. You have learned how to get his attention, how to communicate your message in a calm manner, how to say it clearly, and how to say it concisely. Keep in mind that even Jesus understood that at times, less is more.

These are powerful tools for creating an environment where he will listen to you and take you seriously. Now let's move on to yet another powerful technique in communicating to him—saying it with compassion.

SEVEN

Saying It Compassionately

For no matter how inadequate our unpracticed gestures may seem, they will surely reach into the place that is aching for solace.

DAPHNE ROSE KINGMA

⁂

Tim and Sandy walked into my office and sat down. When I asked how they were doing, Tim offered a boisterous and enthusiastic, "Great. Aren't we?" he said, looking at his wife. "We've had a good week," he said with a smile.

"Sure," Sandy answered, though her response was forced.

Sandy was obviously not doing well. Her face was drawn; she looked tired and sad. Staring at the floor, she averted her eyes from Tim's bright gaze. I sat quietly for a moment, watching them—Tim, cheerful and proud; Sandy, weary and ready to cry. I felt awkward.

Tim and Sandy had been in to see me twice previously. The sessions had been strained. Tim and Sandy had been married for more than 15 years, but they had been tough years. In fact, because of their struggles, Sandy had refused to bring children into the marriage. She confided that she had been unhappy for most of their marriage, primarily due to Tim's alcoholic binges and angry outbursts. He was a difficult man to live with, his moods quickly changing from pleasant and humorous to irritable and irascible. When angry, he would insult her, only to apologize later. He was prone to melancholy that he refused to treat professionally. The alcohol took the edge off for him, but Sandy was left to pick up the pieces in his wake.

Tim wanted to portray their situation in benign terms. He admitted that he drank "a little too much at times," but he insisted he could remedy the problem easily enough. And as for his outbursts, he said he was willing to stop them immediately. According to him, Sandy had no need to be afraid any longer. Not surprisingly, she was not convinced.

In typical fashion, Tim had come to today's session denying the severity of the problem and disregarding Sandy's distress.

"Folks," I said. "I'm puzzled. Tim, you are saying that things are fine. But Sandy, you look very unhappy. What's happening?"

"He doesn't hear me," she said. "I tell him that things are not going well, but he refuses to listen. He wants to believe that everything is fine and that we can move forward. But I am unhappy."

Tim was obviously annoyed. "Didn't we have a good week?" he said. "I didn't drink at all. We went to a movie and spent some great time together. What more do you want?"

"I'm proud of you for not drinking, Tim. But it's only been one week. I've been living with your alcoholism for years. And I'm afraid that you'll start drinking again and that you'll lose your temper like you always do. I can't live like this."

"So even though I've done what you asked, you're saying it's over? Just like that?"

Tim stared angrily at Sandy. He seemed frightened and began quizzing Sandy about her future intentions. He wanted answers. He wanted reassurance that his recent efforts would result in a guarantee that she would not leave him.

"Please listen to me, Tim. You need help for your alcoholism. I can see how hard it is for you to put the bottle down.

You also need counseling for your anger problems. You probably need to be on antidepressants. But I'm tired of talking to you about these issues. You refuse to go to the doctor. You have refused to go to counseling for years. Now, when I am absolutely exhausted and depressed, you want me to snap out of it because you're making an effort. I need some time to think about things, and you need to make some changes in your life."

Silence fell over the room. I felt their pain. A marriage in shambles. A union of two souls now held together by a thread. Both understood that the lives and comforts they had built together were hanging in the balance. Both feared that their frayed bond could unravel at any time.

Sandy's words, spoken with a mixture of candor and compassion that were new for her, had hit the mark. Tim seemed to realize how desperate things had become. He could no longer hide behind a veil of denial; Sandy was no longer willing to enable him.

What do I say to a couple in these desperate circumstances? What hope can I possibly offer them? Platitudes would be an insult to the pain they felt. Both wanted hope: Tim wanted to know that Sandy would not ask for a separation; Sandy wanted to know that she could create a happy life for herself, with or without Tim.

I knew that Sandy was considering a separation—an action powerful enough to make Tim see that the situation was desperate. Something to convince him that he could no longer make promises and then renege on them. "What do you feel like you need, Sandy? What are you asking for today?"

Tears filled her eyes as she slumped in her chair. Tim and I braced ourselves for her answer. All of Tim's initial brightness was gone.

"I'd like a separation, Tim. I don't want to hurt you, but I need some time to think about things. I need to see that you're serious about the changes you need to make. I need to live in a world free from alcohol and anger. Will you work with me so that we can have a peaceful separation, or are you going to make it hard on me?"

There it was. She had dropped the bomb. Tim drooped farther into his chair, looking as deflated as a punctured tire. A few moments before, he had been robust, confident, and optimistic. Now he winced with pain and uncertainty. Sandy's words had hit their mark.

He knew now that she was serious.

Disarming Compassion

Tim was obviously angry with Sandy, but he also knew she felt terrible about her decision. He could see her anguish. She had not scolded him or put him down. She had not recounted the years of turmoil she had endured. She had simply told him she needed to live in a world free from alcohol and anger. That was it. She could tolerate other foibles; she was willing to struggle with him through his depression. But she had to be guaranteed a world without the vicissitudes of anger and alcohol. Anything else could be navigated—but not the two big As.

Compassion can be disarming. It always has been. For that reason, when we parent children, we would do well to follow the principles outlined by authors Foster Cline and Jim Fay in their well-respected book *Parenting with Love and Logic.* They postulate that children learn responsibility much more effectively if parents mete out natural consequences with compassion. Cline and Fay say that rather than letting "I told you so" lectures roll off our tongues so easily, we should let consequences and a compassionate word be the teachers.

Their program is designed for children, but I have found it equally effective when working with adults. Listen again to Sandy's words with Tim.

"I am sorry that this is going to hurt you. I simply cannot live with alcohol and anger in my life any longer. You will have to decide what you are going to do about them. I would like to see you in the future, but you will have to get help for your problems."

Although human compassion falls short of God's heart-changing work, it can accomplish powerful things. Let's consider what compassion can do for the man who needs to listen to and receive a potent message.

First, *compassion links our hearts to the hearts of others.* Compassion lets our spouses know that we understand their plight. We are sensitive to what is happening to them and wish them no harm. We want the best for them, and compassion lets them know this. It helps unlock the door between their heart and ours.

Many of us exhibit a seemingly innate tendency to look at difficult situations as "me against you." We see our spouses as villains. Conversely, compassion says, "We are all in this together." Compassion lets others know that we understand their humanity.

Second, *compassion disarms the listener.* When our spouses know that we care about them and want the best for them, their anger and opposition toward us decrease.

We naturally raise our defenses when we know someone wants something from us. We are especially cautious when we know they want us to change something about ourselves. We all have a built-in mechanism that says, "I am the way I am, and I don't want anyone trying to change me." This, of course, creates barriers between us and those who dare to suggest we need to change.

Third, *compassion makes a statement about our humanity.* It says that I can relate to your situation. Perhaps my scenario is different from yours, but I have lived life too, and I know what it is like to be in your shoes. I know what it is like to be asked to give up something that is dear to me. I know what it is like to be pressed to let go of something that I have come to rely upon in my life. I know what you must be experiencing. This understanding, this compassion, can lower defenses and create a bond between you and your spouse.

Fourth, *compassion changes us.* It is impossible to feel true compassion without being altered by the experience. Compassion softens the heart. It refocuses the senses and makes us more vulnerable. When your man sees your vulnerability, he is more likely to be vulnerable himself.

Finally, *compassion is spiritually bonding.* Compassion is a sacred quality. Our hearts are softened by the Spirit of God, and we can reach out to others from this place of spiritual vulnerability.

If you find yourself in a lonely place, unable to touch the heart of your man, compassion may be the critical link that can bind your heart to his.

The God of All Comfort

Compassion will cut through a lot of excuses, alibis, and obstacles to change, but only God can touch some places in the heart of a man and help him loosen his grip on some things. The Spirit of God can do things that our words, however eloquent they may be, can never do.

The apostle Paul's second letter to the Corinthians reveals important truths about comfort and compassion. Paul's heart is troubled as he offers teaching about suffering and compassion. Let's look at some of his advice. First, he offers a powerful and heartfelt salutation.

"Grace and peace to you from God our Father and the Lord Jesus Christ."

Then Paul moves right into sharing essential truths about compassion and comfort.

> Praise be to the God and Father of our Lord Jesus Christ, the Father of compassion and the God of all comfort, who comforts us in all our troubles, so that we can comfort those in any trouble with the comfort

we ourselves have received from God. For just as the suffering of Christ flow over into our lives, so also through Christ our comfort overflows. If we are distressed, it is for your comfort and salvation; if we are comforted, it is for your comfort, which produces in you patient endurance of the same sufferings we suffer. And our hope for you is firm, because we know that just as you share in our sufferings, so also you share in our comfort (2 Corinthians 1:3-7).

In this short passage, Paul speaks eloquently about compassion, emphasizing the kindness and comfort we have received from Jesus Christ and can share freely with others.

Consider the compassion and comfort you have received from Christ. Consider the blessings you have received. This wellspring of caring will help you say what you want to say to your spouse. When you find it hard to speak with compassion, consider the comfort you have received from Christ and how that same comfort can help you when talking to your partner.

As you think of your spouse and your difficulties with him, you may be tempted to think only of what you are not getting and the frustration that you feel. But you know that beneath his tough exterior, beneath the defenses he erects, he is hurting. He too is in need of compassion. He needs to hear your message couched in kindness.

Consider again some special parts of the passage above: "...the God of all comfort, who comforts us in all our troubles, so that we can comfort those in any trouble with the comfort we ourselves have received from God."

These words are full of expectancy. God has given us the gifts of compassion and comfort and expects us to pass them along.

I remember when my family lost a home to the volcanic ravages of Mount Saint Helens in 1980. In one cataclysmic instant, our world was turned upside down. In the months that followed, we received an outpouring of love from friends, family, and many who did not know us but simply wanted to offer their collective support. We felt the touch of God through these people's cards, letters, gifts, and money. In our emptiness, we were filled up with blessings from many people we knew and many we didn't. Because of their kindness, we developed a feeling of solidarity with others in our community.

God's goodness allows me to offer goodness back to others, not because they "deserve" this goodness but because I am called to offer comfort to others in their troubles as I have received comfort in mine. Similarly, in marriage we have opportunities to step aside from our concerns with self and speak compassionately. We can try to meet our partner's needs even as we ask for our needs to be met. We learn to offer compassion even as we ask our partner to change his life.

Resistance to Compassion

"But I don't *feel* compassionate! I am so upset I want to spit," Dee said. "I don't want to manufacture compassion just so Jeff will hear me. That's ridiculous."

Her words had a rough, painful edge. They were the words of a woman who had struggled in her marriage for several years and was now considering divorce. She had tried everything she knew to reach her husband but to no avail. She wanted him to take a more active role in addressing their financial problems but felt patronized when he gave her simplistic answers and continued ringing up credit card debt. She screamed at him, lectured him, and even left him once because of his compulsive spending. Still, she felt that he didn't understand her needs.

Dee was a powerful woman with a commanding six-foot frame. She was well aware of her ability to intimidate and was abrupt when she spoke to me. Wearing jeans and a sweatshirt, her salty language and no-nonsense style reflected a life spent with working men. She worked as an operator at a local paper mill and made it clear that she could carry her own in a "man's world." Twenty-five years of millwork had hardened her hands, body, and temperament. But the tenacious personality that won the respect of the men with whom she worked had taken a toll on her marriage.

Beneath Dee's calloused hands and muscled exterior was a wounded woman. With great reluctance, she revealed how much she hurt, how distant she and her husband of 20 years, Jeff, had grown from each other.

"I hate it when I cry," she said, dabbing at her eyes. "I don't want to let him see how much he hurts me."

"Why is that?" I asked.

"He hates to see me cry," she said. "He tells me to quit it. So I have learned to just keep it in. But I'm not going to keep living like this. He is going to get some news that he is not going to like. He might love me, but I feel separate from him."

"Well, if you can't cry in front of him, and he is uncomfortable with your pain, as well as his, I can imagine that a lot goes unspoken between you two."

"Yep," she said firmly. "The communication is pretty dry at this point in our lives. 'Pass the salt' is as intimate as we get."

"But you'd like to give it one last effort to reach him? You'd like to save this marriage?"

"Yes, I would. He's a soft man, underneath. And I guess I'm softer than I like to admit too. I'm willing to do whatever it takes to get my message to him."

"I think there are some things we can try that might encourage him to stand up and listen."

With that, Dee and I reviewed some of the things that we've discussed in this book. We focused on trying to talk compassionately, without aggression, which was a definite change for her. We talked about tuning in to her husband's pain, knowing that underneath his macho exterior was a man who was no happier in their marriage than she. We surmised that an injured, rebellious child inside of Jeff might be the source of his struggle with money. The task was to find that vulnerable part of him. She needed to find a way to get beyond her anger so that she could speak compassionately to him.

Change was hard for Dee. She had developed character traits that worked for her on the job but were not effective in her marriage. On the positive side, she wanted to soften her style. With weeks of practice, Dee slowly learned to talk to Jeff compassionately. She was able to communicate with him in a less demanding manner, and he responded positively. Together, they were able to reach agreement about their problems and how to solve them. Jeff emphasized that he hated being "talked down" to and appreciated Dee's efforts to approach him in a calmer, kinder manner.

Making Room for Compassion

Getting your man's attention is not enough. Speaking clearly, as important as that is, isn't enough. Speaking concisely, though that is certainly a powerful tool, isn't even enough. We must also make room for compassion. What does that mean?

Making room for compassion is difficult when negative emotion clouds the air between you and your spouse. This emotional fog only creates distance between you and him.

Only after weeks of work could Dee approach Jeff with compassion. Dee had to find ways to set her incredible frustration, anger, and hurt aside and make room for compassion. She had to "compartmentalize" her feelings of betrayal and anger—an essential skill for all intimate relationships. When Dee looked critically at her interactions with Jeff, she saw how often she let her resentment slip out. She had fallen into a habit of rehearsing her anger, which only served to increase its intensity. She reviewed in her mind all the things Jeff had done wrong during their marriage, including all the embarrassing moments and her "right" to feel angry. However, Dee began to realize that expressing her righteous indignation only created a huge barrier.

It often clouded her perception of Jeff and generated even more resentment toward him. It created a formidable hindrance to intimacy between them and reduced her motivation to speak compassionately toward him.

If Dee had any hope of creating a more hospitable climate for negotiation, she had to set her emotions aside and find a way to speak compassionately and listen compassionately to his story. This was her only way of breaking their impasse. She had nothing to lose and everything to gain.

By setting her anger and hurt aside, she was able to create room for compassion. By imagining that she was putting those feelings in a container and placing them on a shelf, she was able to listen more effectively to his side of the story. She was able to state her feelings more kindly.

Specifically, Dee was able to talk to her husband about her feelings with an understanding that he did not spend money to hurt her.

They agreed that he had a problem with compulsive behavior that would require certain actions, such as destroying his credit cards, at least for a season. When Dee spoke to Jeff compassionately, he did not feel controlled or have the need to rebel against her authoritarian style. She was able to speak to the part of him that hated the financial debt as much as she did. They were now trying to solve a problem together.

Sharing the Problem

One sure way to create room for compassion is to see every marriage problem as a joint problem. You may be tempted to blame your partner, but you will make much more progress if you see the problem as something you created together and something you can remedy together.

Not surprisingly, creating the mind-set that "this is *our* problem" can be challenging.

Recently, I had the opportunity to face once again that part of me that likes to be right. I have always taken great pride in my ability to work out interpersonal problems with others but have never wanted to face my pride and see it for the sin that it is. I have always rationalized my "being right" by saying to myself, *I know more about fair fighting than other people. I have the right to set the tone of the disagreement and do things my way.*

Recently, in a "fight," a friend pointed out my self-righteousness.

"What gives you the right to set the direction for our fight?" she asked.

"I know a lot about fair fighting, and these are fair-fight rules," I replied.

"But that doesn't explain why we have to do things your way. That way you win, and I lose. It doesn't seem fair to me."

Again, I protested, falling back on my superior training and expertise. I have written books on the topic, I told myself. But I also knew that I tended to feel vulnerable when things were not going my way. I felt out of control. I disliked the tension that arose when conflicts were left unfinished, and I had the skills (read that as *manipulation!*) to end them.

I was not able to concede her point at the time. Only in retrospect could I see that though I had a valid point—I did have extensive training and expertise—I had no reason to always insist on doing things my way. Instead, we needed to agree upon the rules for our fighting and proceed in a way that would satisfy both of us—and it worked!

Sharing the problem is a powerful technique. Choosing to not fall back on "being right" will create an abundance of goodwill in your relationship. It will provide the foundation for speaking to your partner compassionately.

Dr. Susan Jeffers, author of *Opening Our Hearts to Men,* offers similar advice:

In order to let go of the need to be right, it is necessary to soothe that place within that feels so threatened, which, as we all know, isn't so easy to do. What keeps us feeling inferior and unsure of ourselves is our inner Chatterbox—that negative voice within that fills us with messages of gloom and doom and, in some way or another, always tries to convince us that we really are not good enough.[1]

To share the problem—especially when every fiber of your being screams, *Blame him! It's his fault!*—is not easy. In fact, Jeffers lists many silent payoffs for holding on to self-righteousness. See if you can relate with any of them:

- It gives women a sense of superiority at a time when self-esteem is low.
- It keeps women from having to look in the mirror and ask, *How might I have contributed to the circumstances in my life that don't work?*
- It allows women to blame others, thus keeping them "victims" so they don't have to take action.
- It serves as self-talk at a time when a part of them needs to be convinced.[2]

Jeffers believes, as do I, that one of the most powerful ways to silence the inner chatterbox is through spirituality. In the natural realm, the realm of the EGO—Easing God Out—we will never be able to fully relinquish our desire to be right and win. The ego wants control, the ego wants to be right, the ego craves feelings of superiority, and the ego protects our more vulnerable nature.

But when we let go of our immature, selfish desires, we are able to let the Spirit of God work in our circumstances. In our spiritual nature, we can see our part in the problem and work with our spouse cooperatively.

A Compassionate Change of Spirit

Sometimes we try to paste Band-Aids on problems rather than going deeper to find their causes. Sometimes we tell ourselves small lies in order to avoid the pain of telling ourselves the truth. The same obstacle can stand in the way when we attempt to say what we have to say with compassion. Try as we might, if we don't have a change of spirit, or a spiritual change, we will simply be putting a Band-Aid on the problem.

Paul Tournier, the famous Swiss physician and theologian, speaks at length about this problem. In his wonderful book *To Understand Each Other,* Tournier agrees, along with Jeffers and countless others, that we must learn to relate to one another from a spiritual basis. We must change our nature, which compels us to compete and strive and gain a one-up position on our partners.

> Psychology thus may reveal problems and suggest wise measures to be taken. But the real solution of problems demands a more profound change, one of a spiritual nature. It is this change in spirit which the Bible calls "metanoia," or "repentance": change of spirit and also self-examination, humiliation, a conscious acceptance of responsibilities hitherto ignored....We need a breath of fresh air, the breath of God's Spirit. No other force in the world can touch a man more deeply in his heart and make him more apt, at last, at understanding others. He sees his responsibilities. He understands that he is hurting the person he did not understand. He realizes that failure to understand and unwillingness to seek understanding are what caused his withdrawal into blind self-centeredness.[3]

I doubt that many of us would argue with Tournier. We know that being compassionate, especially in the face of conflict, requires something superhuman of us. In fact, it requires something spiritual. It requires spiritual, God-given help. It requires a denouncement of our selfish desires and a willingness to humble ourselves.

As the apostle Paul says, "Do not think of yourself more highly than you ought, but rather think of yourself with sober judgment, in accordance with the measure of faith God has given you" (Romans 12:3).

Adding sober judgment to our abilities, through the work of the Spirit, we are equipped to speak compassionately. Even when we don't naturally feel compassionate, we are able to transcend our selfish nature through the inner work of the Spirit. We watched both Sandy and Dee learn this skill, even though they had to go against their natural tendencies. We watched how candor and compassion provided an effective strategy for being heard.

All of us are able to find compassion when we look for it, knowing that we have been created equally and have been given the measure of faith necessary to speak compassionately to our partner.

Let's now move forward with another critical skill for getting your message to your man: speaking consistently.

EIGHT

Saying It Consistently

My object in living is to unite
My avocation and my vocation
As my two eyes make one in sight.
Only where love and need are one,
And the work is play for mortal stakes
Is the deed ever really done
For Heaven and the future's sakes.

ROBERT FROST

﷼ ❀ ﷼

Puget Sound and the coastline of Washington State have always cast a spell over me. I can sit and watch the tides roll in and out for hours. Living near the water's edge at my island getaway, I have learned respect for the surf. The tides are not only predictable but also powerful. A stroll along the beach reveals treasures, products of the pounding surf. Pieces of glass, water-worn, lose their edges. Shells are ground smooth by the incessant water. The unceasing waves pulverize rocks. Evidence of travelers here yesterday has been washed clean by the tides.

I have learned to watch my step because I know the tide will inexorably come in, possibly stranding me in places I do not care to be. I have learned the potency of riptides; several people are killed every year not far from my home because they fail to respect the hidden forces. One should never take the tidal eddies, rips, and currents for granted.

We can learn many lessons from the tides. Perhaps most important is recognizing the power of consistency. The predictability and sureness of the sea comforts me. When everything else in life seems unstable, chaotic, and unpredictable, the fixed forces ordained by the Creator assure me of His faithfulness. We can depend on Him.

Consider for a moment the power of consistency. Reflect back on those people you knew to be consistent. They were unflinching, unwavering, undeniable. Perhaps they were parents or grandparents or church leaders. In every case, you always knew where you stood with them. You knew what you could expect from them, and they were perfectly clear about what they expected from you. Perhaps, like me, you reflect back on these individuals with respect for their strength and determination.

My childhood was nearly idyllic. I did not think so at the time, but now I see how fortunate I was. One of the reasons my collection of childhood memories is so favorable is that I was surrounded by consistency. My parents came from "the old school"—that is, they meant what they said. They were firm, consistent, and loving. They were steadfast. Their life messages communicated certainty to their five children. Neither parent could be swayed from his or her resolution. What they said was fixed. They expected us to understand and follow through with directives. No ifs, ands, or buts.

My mother was a second-generation Swede, raised on hard work and discipline. Her parents were part of the wave of Swedish immigrants who came to America in the late 1800s, seeking their fortune and finding at least some of it through their hard work. Mom, understandably, passed along some of this mind-set about hard work to us children. Chores were considered as good for growing children as spinach and broccoli. Add to that three square meals of church per week, along with heavy doses of love, and her children were bound to turn out all right. Make no mistake, however; my mother expected us to listen to her and respect her. And so we did.

My father also came from Scandinavian stock—more Norwegian than Swede, however, which created a humorous rivalry and banter between my parents. He too raised us to be mindful of our parents' directives. Like our mother, he expected us children to listen carefully to what he said and to follow his rules. He created a wonderful mixture of consistency and love. He added a strong dose of fun to keep the mood light. But we knew that his word, like my mother's, was to be taken seriously.

Though my parents were clear about rules and the structure they chose for our family, I was intent on testing the limits. I understood the fences they put up for the family, but I wondered if I might sneak around them, dig under them, or leap over them. At times, I imagined myself superior to my parents' ways of doing things. In my self-centered view of the world, I thought that I knew better. So I proceeded to try things on my own, to test their consistency.

My adolescent years were filled with escapades that involved trying to skirt my parents' protective restrictions. Sneaking out the basement window to join my friends invariably led to serious consequences. Attempts to extend established curfews were consistently met with firm denials. Most of the time, my delinquency was caught in the act, and I was disciplined appropriately. When I offered various explanations to avoid personal responsibility, my parents maintained their consistency. No excuses were acceptable. My efforts to deny the problem, blame others, and offer weak arguments were always met with stout resolve.

"David, what you did was wrong," my mother would tell me. "You made a poor choice. I am sorry, but now you won't be able to spend the night at Mike's house this weekend. Maybe you'll make a different choice next time."

Ouch! Clear, compassionate, consistent limits met me head-on every time I tried to dodge responsibility. I was invariably faced with the repercussions of my actions. Year after year, I attempted to dodge these boundaries. Year after year, I failed. I learned powerful lessons.

Together, my parents provided an environment built on strong moral and spiritual values. Together, they created a world that was predictable and consistent. We knew what was expected of us, and we knew that if we chose to ignore those expectations, which we did at times, we would experience the consequences.

Now that I am in midlife, I am convinced that the consistent world they created formed much of the basis for the general happiness I enjoy today. I never take their consistency for granted. It is a hallmark of healthy individuals.

Kate and Daniel

If consistency is good for growing boys and girls, how important is it for growing adults? Let me illustrate using an example of inconsistency, which, unfortunately, is all too familiar in many marriages.

Kate and Daniel had been married 16 years when they came to see me after one of Daniel's many extramarital affairs had come to light. Infidelity was the dominant feature of their troubled relationship—and episodes of pornography use. Daniel seemed able to stay free from extramarital entanglements and pornography for several years—just long enough for Kate to recover from the previous episode—and then another affair would occur. This time, according to Kate, would be the last. She had said that many times before, but she had informed Daniel that she now wanted to get to the root of the problem. She would accept nothing less than hard work and complete fidelity.

Daniel was no typical carouser, if such a thing exists. He was a likeable, hard-working attorney with a strong faith in God. Of modest build, with full, curly hair, Daniel was beginning to gray around the temples. While friendly enough, Daniel appeared serious and tense. He approached counseling with the same tempo he maintained at work—he wanted to get to the issues, especially the issue of saving his marriage.

Daniel prided himself in working long hours, though as he grew older, the hours seemed to deplete his limited energy. He was a well-respected lawyer, sought after for his expertise in family law. In talking to Daniel about his affairs, he offered little in the way of explanation. He seemed as perplexed about why he was unfaithful as his wife.

Kate was a strong woman in her own right. She worked as the head librarian at the local library. She was skilled verbally and was impatient, frustrated, and angry about Daniel's cheating. She wanted to understand his infidelity, and her search for the truth seemed more important to her than setting healthy boundaries in her marriage. She seemed to believe that by understanding Daniel's unfaithfulness, she could prevent him from doing it again. Her resolve to find the answers also kept her intense grief at bay.

Kate had been anything but consistent with Daniel. She made threats and then failed to follow through with them. She promised to never tolerate another affair, only to back down when it occurred. She lectured Daniel, scolded him, and threatened him. At times she slipped into a tirade against him, calling him derogatory names. But she was never consistent in her message. Perhaps Daniel knew that Kate would not follow through on her promises. Perhaps he knew that she was uncertain of her position.

Kate certainly cannot be criticized for her efforts. She is doing what has come naturally to her for years. She has a lot to lose if she maintains consistency in her marriage. After all, should she follow through with her limits, if she decides that a boundary without consequences is no boundary at all, she may be faced with the most difficult decision of her lifetime. She may have to decide that Daniel cannot continue to act out and still be married to her. She may decide that she will separate from him if he refuses to get to the bottom of his behavior and make radical changes. She has considered that radical change could risk losing her financial safety, the country club membership, and even her home. Still, something needed to change.

I have said in one of my earlier books, *Men Just Don't Get It—But They Can*, that real change requires real action. Band-Aids do not work. Kate had used Band-Aids for years. Let's listen to her explain how she has responded to Daniel in the past. You will notice her lack of clarity and consistency.

"I've known about Daniel's cheating for a long time. He has cheated at least five times that I know about, possibly more. Each time, he promises never to do it again, and I've always accepted that. But I have never really believed him, and I guess I've been lying to myself.

"I've known that he's not really facing his issues. I've known that he should be in counseling to understand and deal with his apparent sexual addiction. But I've always wanted to believe that he can fix this thing himself, like he promises. I realize that when I threaten to leave him if he does it again, and then he does it and I do nothing, I lose his respect. Over the years, I've lost respect for him, and he's lost respect for me."

As you might suspect, Kate required as much counseling as Daniel. While we emotionally rail against him for his lack of respect for his wife and the covenantal integrity of marriage, we also want to shout at Kate, "Don't keep tolerating his abuse. Take a firm stand. If he doesn't get serious counseling, he will only hurt you again. Be strong. Set a firm boundary so that your marriage can not only survive, but thrive. The road ahead will be painful, but both of you can experience healing."

Realistically, most of us could not be that firm, regardless of the promises we make to the contrary. The Kate in all of us commonly says one thing and does another. We often talk boldly but act frightened and confused. Being consistent in our conversations with others is difficult, especially when doing so means risking love and relationship.

The Difficulty with Inconsistency

Kate is like many of us. Her pattern of inconsistency is destroying her life. Many of us are living inconsistently as well. We say one thing and then do another. We establish a boundary and then fail to stay true to what we have said. Let's look a little closer at how this works.

First, *we give inconsistent messages to our partners.* We tell them that we mean business, that our boundaries are firm, but then we fail to follow through when the boundary is breached. This leaves our spouses confused as to what to believe. Should they believe that we really do mean business, or should they believe that they can get away with anything they want because we fear the consequences of sticking to our guns?

Second, *we are emotionally inconsistent with ourselves.* Because we are not truly honest with ourselves, we fail to be honest with others about what is really bothering us. With a foundation of emotional dishonesty, we can never be consistent with others.

Virginia Satir, renowned family therapist, emphasized the importance of being emotionally honest with ourselves. In her book *Making Contact,* she said, "Being emotionally honest, is the heart of making contact....Most people take emotional dishonesty for granted and are unaware that anything else is possible. They really think they are doing what they ought to do and then suffer unnecessarily as a result."[1]

Kate was afraid of being honest with herself. She was afraid of facing the truth about how devastated she really was by Daniel's unfaithfulness. When alone, in the quiet of her home, she often felt so wracked with pain that she was frightened, and she pushed away from the powerful emotions. Emotional honesty would probably lead to change, and that was frightening to her. *What if Daniel refuses to change?* she wondered.

Third, *we fear being consistent.* Being consistent means that we will have to follow through with consequences. Consistency propels us in a direction; it is terribly risky business. If we say what we mean and mean what we say, we will be making a profound statement. Others will take us seriously. We will be "out there" for others to reject, support, ridicule, or applaud. Our neck will be on the line. Consistency requires courage.

Fourth, *being inconsistent translates into a lack of clarity.* We have already talked about the importance of being clear with our spouses. We cannot be consistent without being clear. We must spend time thinking through exactly what we feel, think, and want. We must be clear with ourselves and others. This will take work. It will take due diligence.

Finally, *inconsistency results in impotence.* Being consistent is like having a personal mission statement. It directs our lives. It unifies our diverse feelings and the messages we send to others. Inconsistency produces the opposite results. Our message is diluted. Our power and influence are weakened. When that occurs, we shouldn't be surprised that other people don't take us seriously.

David Whyte, author of the book *The Heart Aroused,* talked at length about being clear in his mission. Frustrated for years by confusion and lack of direction, meandering from job to job, he spent much time listening to his heart, his passions, for a consistent message. He worked long and hard on being consistent in his life. He searched for ways to bring his motives in line with his mission. He sought strategies for bringing his actions in line with his goals.

> Everything I needed for this outrageous step into a new life, including my innocent and childlike emulation of Jacques Cousteau, had been done out of a kind of sheer joy. It was exactly what I loved most that qualified me for my next step....I determined at that moment never to lose faith in those personal passions and desires that had led me to this oddly miraculous place of fulfillment.[2]

Whyte discovered his life calling and deep satisfaction.

Consistency in Marriage

Kate resolved to change her life, regardless of what Daniel decided to do. She had apparently hit bottom when she came in for counseling. She was suffering and vowed that her suffering would lead to healthy change. She would no longer live from one loss of trust to another, stringing together glimpses of happiness and true connection.

We went to work. Kate and Daniel wanted to save their marriage. Neither wanted a continuation of their current situation. As I worked with Kate and Daniel on their interpersonal issues, we also addressed individual problems they were bringing to the marriage. Kate especially lacked several skills. Perhaps you can relate to her need to guard against several things:

- waffling in her resolve
- defending her position
- becoming easily distracted
- losing her message in emotionality

Kate rejected these and focused on more positive actions:

- being consistent and clear in what she expected from Daniel
- not defending or debating her position
- staying focused
- remaining calm

Kate decided that she needed Daniel to diligently work on his issues in order for her to feel safe in their marriage in the future. She would settle for nothing less. She had thought about it and decided that his excuses, alibis, and rationalizations were not enough consolation for her this time. She needed more. She needed him to do some real work and tackle his issues in counseling. She needed him to understand the triggers leading to "relapse." She needed him to explore ways to be completely faithful in heart and action. She needed him to explore spiritual values and strengths to help him with his issues. This would be the only way she could feel comfortable that the old patterns would not repeat themselves.

Initially, one of Kate's biggest tasks was to avoid being distracted by Daniel's defenses. She had spent countless hours chasing rabbits, listening to irrelevant talk, rather than staying riveted to the topic at hand: Daniel's reprehensible behavior. She had been easily distracted by his defensiveness. And why would he not be defensive? After all, he was being confronted by Kate. She was finally speaking to him clearly, concisely, and consistently. His back was against the wall. He had to choose whether to change or not.

Daniel's work, in the face of Kate's solid position, included accepting responsibility for his actions. Previously able to dance around the issue with excuses, arguments, and alibis, he now found Kate's consistent message a formidable opponent. He could no longer avoid the issue. He had to take complete responsibility for his sexual addiction and irresponsibility and make changes if he wanted to stay married to Kate. It was that simple.

Perhaps you are having difficulty staying focused in your marriage. Perhaps your confrontations are meeting with excuses and other errors in thinking. You know the kind:

- constructing arguments of distraction
- making excuses
- rationalizing
- playing the victim
- blaming someone else

One of the principal tasks when attempting to remain consistent is to avoid distractions. Opportunities to get sidetracked abound. Deceptive rabbit trails seem to pop up out of nowhere, semi-relevant topics tempt us away from the central issues, and half-truths tease us into abandoning the heart of the message we are trying to send.

When preparing to deliver your message, consider using the "broken record" technique. This technique is just as it sounds—saying the same thing over and over again. Here's how it might play out with Kate and Daniel.

Kate: "Daniel, I want you to get help for your ongoing unfaithfulness. Some counseling groups are set up specifically for this problem."

Daniel: "I don't think I have an addiction. I know what I need to do to stop."

Kate: "Perhaps you do, but that is not enough. I want you to enter counseling specifically for your sexual addiction."

Daniel: "I don't want to go for help with a bunch of perverts."

Kate: "I know that it feels embarrassing to you, but I expect you to receive specific treatment for sexual addiction if you want me to stay with you."

Daniel: "Are you threatening me?"

Kate: "If you want to put it that way, yes. I expect you to receive specific help for your sexual addiction."

Staying focused and consistent is the only way through the maze. It is the only sure way to deal with problems. Consistent messages are powerful tools when used with the other techniques offered so far in this book.

Queen Esther

The biblical story of Queen Esther offers us a picture of powerful consistency. You might recall how this woman honed her assertiveness in the crucible of life.

We have no indication that Esther desired power. Perhaps hers started as an ordinary life like yours or mine. She lived under the reign of King Xerxes. The king held a seven-day royal banquet, and while he was "high in spirits from the wine," he wanted to display his wife, Queen Vashti. He gave an order to bring out his queen to show her off to the people. But Queen Vashti wanted none of that and refused to come out. The king burned with anger.

Because of her rebellion, Queen Vashti was deposed, and a search for a new queen began. One woman's poor choice is another's opportunity. The search for a suitable replacement yielded many candidates, but one in particular caught the king's eye. A Jew named Mordecai had raised Esther after her parents' death, and now Esther was taken to the palace as a candidate for queen. Esther found favor with the king and was provided with many beauty treatments.

After the completion of 12 months of treatments, Esther was brought before the king. "And Esther won the favor of everyone who saw her." King Xerxes made her his queen, and everyone in the land celebrated. He gave her a great banquet and even proclaimed a holiday in her honor. Everything was going well—until the plot thickened.

One day, Haman, one of the king's officials, became upset because Mordecai, a Jew, refused to bow down when Haman passed by. Haman was enraged and set out to kill not only Mordecai but all Jews. Haman informed King Xerxes of the problem:

> There is a certain people dispersed and scattered among the peoples in all the provinces of your kingdom whose customs are different from those of all other people and who do not obey the king's laws; it is not in the king's best interest to tolerate them. If it pleases the king, let a decree be issued to destroy them, and I will put ten thousand talents of silver into the royal treasury for the men who carry out this business (Esther 3:8-9).

The king agreed and gave Haman his signet ring to seal the deal.

When the king made this hasty agreement, he did not know that his queen was a Jew. He did not recognize the wickedness of Haman or his ulterior motives to destroy the Jews and elevate himself in the process.

As the story unfolds, Mordecai heard of Haman's evil plot and sent word to Queen Esther, encouraging her to go to the king on behalf of herself and the rest of the Jews. However, she reminded him that no one went to the king without first being summoned. To do so could mean immediate death.

When Esther's words were reported back to Mordecai, he boldly offered his reply—words we would do well to consider:

> Do not think that because you are in the king's house you alone of all the Jews will escape. For if you remain silent at this time, relief and deliverance for the Jews will arise from another place, but you and your father's family will perish. And who knows but that you have come to royal position for such a time as this? (4:13-14).

Mordecai challenges the queen to make a move that could cost her life. He challenges her to consider what is most important to her and to bravely act. He asks Esther to become clear, to become consistent, in the most important message that she will ever deliver to her man—the king.

Esther collects her thoughts. She considers her options. I presume that she prayerfully clarifies the message she wants to give to Mordecai and her king. She then sends word to Mordecai to gather all of the Jews and instructs them to fast for three days in preparation for her encounter with the king. She is ready to put it all on the line. Her final words to Mordecai: "If I perish, I perish."

Queen Esther prepares for her encounter with the king. She approaches him and is received. The king asks what she wants.

She says that she wants the king and Haman to come to a banquet prepared for them. At that banquet, the king again asks what it is that the queen wants. She says she wants the king and Haman to come to another banquet in their honor. The queen is surely setting the stage for a greater request. She is focused, clear, and consistent.

Finally, the time had come. At the second banquet, the king again asks Queen Esther what she wants. Now, fully prepared, she delivers her message. "Spare my people....For I and my people have been sold for destruction and slaughter and annihilation. If we had merely been sold as male and female slaves, I would have kept quiet, because no such distress would justify disturbing the king."

The king is enraged.

"Who is he? Where is the man who has dared to do such a thing?"

Haman's plot is revealed. He is hanged with a noose he had prepared for Mordecai. The queen protests in favor of her people, the Jews, and a new order is signed, saving them. Mordecai is raised to prominence in the kingdom. Queen Esther's bravery is rewarded. Her message has been delivered with sureness and consistency.

Consistency: Our Mission Statement

Laurie Beth Jones' book *The Path* is helpful in this task of creating consistency in your message. She purports that creating a mission statement is a sure way to become clear, convinced, and convincing about what is important. It is a sure way to burn off the dross that surrounds the heart of what we stand for and reveal the pure, consistent message.

> Those that have never known what it's like to feel a passionate commitment to a cause would be catapulted from their couches onto the playing field, tasting the dirt, feeling the sweat and the sting of

tears and having the wind knocked out of them...and
in the process become fully alive.[3]

Wow! Can we become so clear about the message we want
to deliver that we become passionate about it? Can it become
the heart of what is happening to us at a particular time? I think
so. In fact, if the message doesn't take on this kind of passion, I
am afraid it will get lost in a jungle of words—broken, frayed,
insipid words that lose their punch. And that is not what we
want if you are striving to send a powerful message to your man.
About mission statements, Jones says this:

> While mission statements seem only recently to
> have sprung into the public consciousness, they
> have, in fact, been around for centuries. One of the
> most powerful and influential leaders of all time
> articulated his mission statement in a single sen-
> tence two thousand years ago: "I have come that
> they might have life, and have it more abundantly."
> Every activity he undertook—whether turning
> water into wine, playing with children, holding sem-
> inars by the sea, or challenging the current religious
> system—was a result of his mission statement.[4]

And what does all of this have to do with consistency? It is
this. Out of our personal mission statement comes the passion
to send a powerful message. It helps us synthesize what is truly
important. It shaves off the unnecessary elements of the message and gets to the heart of things.

What exactly do you want to say? How can you say it as
clearly, concisely, compassionately, and consistently as possible? If you waver, if you become distracted and change topics,
and if you fail to follow through on what you have said you will
do, your message lacks potency.

The mission statement, the distillation of complex matters
into a few simple sentences, repeated as often as necessary, is an

influential tool. Jones says, "A personal mission statement acts as both a harness and a sword—harnessing you to what is true about your life, and cutting away all that is false."[5]

Kate decided that her mission was to expect complete sexual faithfulness from Daniel, making no excuses for his past behavior. She expected him to pursue an in-depth path of healing with no quick-fix remedies. As she became clearer and more consistent, she found Daniel willing to make positive changes, and at this time, they are doing well. He is facing his problems and has greater respect for Kate for being strong.

As you continue on your path of speaking firmly to your man, consider how you might clarify your message. Consider how you might bring passion to what you want to say without being distracted by emotion.

The passion you bring to this moment will be harnessed, focused. It will drive your message. It will help you stay the course, saying again and again, as often as needed, exactly what you need from your man. And you will find it to be effective.

Now we move forward to our next powerful tool for getting your message to your man: saying it with conviction.

NINE

Saying It with Conviction

To do justice, love mercy, and walk humbly.
That is what I've learned from life.

VERNON JORDAN

ఠఇ ✿ ఞఌ

Alexander sat on the floor of his room, sulking. He peered at the posters tacked on the wall, the rumpled stack of comic books in the corner, and the stuffed animals plopped on his bed. Looking up at the ceiling, he told himself that his parents could never force him to pack his baseball mitt, his I LOVE DINO-SAURS sweatshirt, or his red cowboy boots. His parents were busy packing things in another room, but Alexander spoke as though they could hear him. "I'm not packing," he said. "I'm not going to move."

Alexander is going through a crisis. As an 11-year-old boy who has grown accustomed to his life, he feels threatened. He sees his idyllic world slipping away. Things he has treasured. Friends he has grown to love. A life that is so important to him.

Judith Viorst shares Alexander's sentiments about moving in one of her popular children's books, *Alexander, Who's Not (Do You Hear Me? I Mean It!) Going to Move.* It is a heartbreaking story of a boy who meets one of life's challenges, the prospect

149

of leaving friends and familiarity, with resolve and inner conviction. When told that his family will be leaving because of a change in his father's career, he responds, "I'm not—do you hear me? I mean it!—going to move."

Although his parents lovingly tried to encourage him by laying out all the benefits of moving and assuring him that he would eventually make new friends, Alexander was not buying it. He was emphatic that he would not be moving with the family. "Never. Not ever. No way. Uh-uh. N.O....I know places to hide where they'll never find me. I'd rather have poison ivy than have to move."[1]

While we sympathize with Alexander's plight and understand the struggles that accompany change, we also admire Alexander's resolve—stubbornness from his parents' perspective, I suppose—to make a statement based on his feelings and beliefs. He is clear, concise, and convincing, and he speaks with conviction. How can we not smile at his determination? Clearly arguing with this boy will have little impact.

Another example of conviction can be found at the other end of the age spectrum in the person of Mahatma Gandhi. A picture of him is indelibly imprinted on our minds, made popular by the movie of the same name starring Ben Kingsley: balding, sinewy, wearing round glasses, soft and subtle in white. His mission was clear, his voice strong with inner conviction. His desire was to free India from British rule, but to do so with nonviolent means. This, of course, would be no small task.

Gandhi was a small man with a soft voice. His physical presence would not immediately command attention. But what he lacked in height and girth, he more than made up for with powerful ideas, force of thought, and inner conviction. What he lacked in physical presence, he surpassed with quiet, laser-like belief.

Born to the Vaishya caste, only a small step above the working class, Gandhi did not grow up accustomed to privilege. The name *Gandhi* means "grocer," apparently a trade in the family history. Questioning authority apparently ran in the family as well, as his grandfather and father were both forced out of civil positions, apparently due to their convictions and activism.

Gandhi studied law in Britain, but he failed to develop a legal practice. Humbled by his lack of success, he sympathized with the working class. He was further humiliated in South Africa, where he worked for 20 years and was mobbed and beaten on numerous occasions.

Gandhi was certainly not alone in believing that India should be free from British rule. However, unlike his more aggressive contemporaries, he felt that war against Britain should be waged peacefully. This short, simple man stood firm in his convictions and gradually became what the United States Secretary of State General George C. Marshall called "the spokesman for the conscience of all mankind."[2]

More than anyone else, Gandhi is responsible for establishing his country's freedom through nonviolence. He did it through the use of *satyagraha*—a Sanskrit term he coined meaning "truth and persistence." It was a method of direct social action based upon principles of courage, nonviolence, and truth. *Satyagraha* emphasizes that the way people behave is more important than what they achieve. Certainly capable of great success in other fields, he chose to live simply and adhere to his convictions. Gandhi's life was guided by the search for truth, and he lived and died according to his courage and conviction.

More recently, our nation was stirred by the death of President Ronald Reagan. Not since the death of President Kennedy have so many crowded into the streets, shared a poignant and painful moment, lined up in the Capitol Rotunda, and responded in such a public way. Not in 50 years have we seen so much affection and admiration given to one person. But clearly the admiration was not meant for him alone. His life was more than the sum of his political accomplishments. We, as a nation, were touched by more than a movie star turned governor turned president.

As I watched the newscasts and pageantry associated with President Reagan's funeral, I saw something deeper. His wife, Nancy Reagan, received well-deserved accolades for her deep convictions and for standing as a pillar of strength. What did we see that touched us so deeply?

We noticed that she had been away from the public eye for a long time. Doing what? Caring for her ailing husband. Nancy all but put her life aside while President Reagan suffered from the ravages of Alzheimer's disease. She nurtured him, tended to him, cared for him. A woman with a reputation of being a bit "hard" spent years being soft and loving to a man who was probably incapable of offering anything in return. We wonder if we would be capable of making the same sacrifices.

In this most public of ceremonies, our nation caught a glimpse of what she must have experienced nurturing her man through a slow and agonizing death caused by Alzheimer's. We reflect upon the gritty resolve, the fierce conviction that convinced her not only to stay with her husband but also to singularly focus on keeping him as healthy and happy as possible under the circumstances. Americans understandably admire this incredible woman who walked alongside her man for more than 50 years.

How did she do it? "You just do it," she said. "You take each day as it comes and put one foot in front of the other." While she makes this process sound simple enough, we know that it is not that simple. We know that these actions stem from the power of inner resolve. Her convictions determined that she would stand by her man through the heady days of love letters and giddy flirtation, through the glory years of movies and Hollywood, through the power years of the presidency, and through the despairing days of illness and ultimate death. The solid foundation of love created the determination that carried her through to the end.

Weak Words

When I first saw Deidre, she exhibited symptoms of depression. A short, overweight woman in her early forties, she wore a stylish dress. She had several rings on her polished fingers and bracelets on her wrists. She spoke clearly, enunciating her words as she told me how she had struggled with depression for years and how her problems had grown worse in the past year due to severe marital conflict. She told me that her sleep was fitful, her mood deflated, her energy almost gone. It was all she could do to make it to work each day at the local hospital where she was an admitting clerk.

"Why have things taken such a turn recently?" I asked.

"My husband, Tom, stays away on road trips for long periods of time. I think he is cheating on me," she said sullenly.

"Do you have any evidence of that?"

"Well, there really isn't any evidence. I just feel it. He's often away on business, he doesn't call me, and he doesn't act like he loves me when he's home. When I question him about these things he gets angry and defensive. He tells me I'm insecure and need counseling."

Deidre sat quietly, waiting for my response. She fidgeted with the bracelets on her wrist.

"Have you talked to Tom about your feelings?" I said. "I mean, really talked to him? Have you two discussed your problems? Are you working on things?"

"No, not really. I don't know what to say to him. I just feel so distant from him. When I think about Tom being away so much, and how we are so far apart when he is home, I feel hurt and angry. I think that just pushes him away all the more. He is self-confident and always has an answer for anything I might say. He dismisses my concerns, calling them trivial."

"Tell me why he is away so much," I said.

"He works in the telecommunications field. I really don't know exactly what he does, but he's gone three nights a week."

I spent the balance of the session exploring Deidre's relationship with her husband of ten years and analyzing the patterns of communication they had developed. It became clear that she and Tom did not communicate effectively. Deidre was passively avoidant, while Tom seemed, by her description, to be arrogant and self-centered. She said that he had little time or interest in hearing about her struggles. She thought that Tom was as unhappy as she, but he also failed to take action to address their problems. I discovered little evidence of an affair, though their relationship was on target for something bad to happen.

Confusion was just below the surface of Deidre's depression. She did not know what she thought anymore. She had lost her inner convictions. She thought that Tom traveled too much and that he did not show her enough attention when he was home, but he always countered her arguments. Whenever she did raise a concern, he had a ready defense that weakened her views. As a result, she doubted what she saw, felt, and believed. She doubted herself.

Even more significant was Deidre's history. She had grown up in a home where her father, a longshoreman, drank excessively. Her mother stayed home and played the dutiful, unhappy martyr. Her mother never, as far as Deidre knew, confronted her father about his drinking. She complained at times to Deidre but also told her that "good wives put up with some things for the sake of their marriage." Deidre seemed to be replaying what she had learned at home, putting up with dysfunctional behavior "because that is what women do"—even if it leads to unhappiness and a failing marriage.

My initial work with Deidre was to help her find her lost voice. She had stifled her feelings and beliefs for so long that she was unsure of what she felt or believed. She had been "lost" in her family of origin and now found herself passively following old patterns, long outdated.

I asked Deidre to begin journaling. I wanted her to write several paragraphs every day and to write out several things:

- how she felt about what was happening
- what she would like to do differently
- how she could express herself

I also told her to dare to disagree and to note what happened when she did.

Why did I want Deidre to begin journaling? I have found journaling to be a powerful tool in exploring what we think and feel about our lives. I think it is also a valuable way to listen to what God might be saying to us and to perceive His directions for our lives. In addition, journaling is a way to create a relationship with ourselves that may have diminished over time. It is a powerful technique in understanding our inner convictions—those things that are important to us, that define us, that set our lives in the direction that they need to go.

When Conviction Vanishes

Take note of a three-year-old in a typical family. Watch as she moves through her world, exploring, searching, questioning. Notice her delight as she solves problems, creates new things, and begins to understand cause-effect relationships. Her world is growing, and her abilities expand daily.

In her healthy family, this three-year-old is encouraged to explore her world and to notice the connection between things. She is allowed to feel what she feels, think what she thinks, know what she knows. Are her perceptions entirely correct? Of course not. But she begins to have convictions as a natural outgrowth of living and exploring her world.

Was Alexander "right" in saying that he was never going to move, "no way, uh-uh, not now, not ever"? In his healthy family, he was able to have those thoughts and to maintain his convictions. He was not able to have anything he wanted, but he could have his convictions. They were natural and certainly understandable.

If convictions are natural and perhaps even God-given at times, what has happened to Deidre? What stops her from saying what she wants to say? Why doesn't she stand up to Tom and set some boundaries that will help her feel more secure?

Perhaps your story has some similarities to Deidre's. Perhaps you have lost your inner convictions. Perhaps you have been talked out of thinking what you think, knowing what you know, or feeling what you feel. How does that typically happen?

First, *other people may be threatened by what we believe.* Not everyone will champion our point of view. Feeling threatened, they will try to dismiss what we hold to be important.

We do not know what was happening in Tom's world. We cannot say that he was having an affair or even that he was traveling too much. We can only be sure that Deidre was fearful that he was having an affair. We know that she felt insecure and unhappy about his travel. These are true and indisputable for her.

Others may be threatened by our values, beliefs, and convictions. That's okay. Good communication allows each person to have his or her beliefs and feelings without being dismissed or talked out of them. Perceptions are very personal aspects of our personhood. Others dare not tell us to think differently than we think.

Second, *we may be threatened by what we believe.* When we take a stand, when we offer our perceptions, we put something on the line. We stick our necks out, and we become vulnerable.

Deidre had been ridiculed for her perceptions. But she had also doubted them. Eleanor Roosevelt once said, "No one can make me feel bad about myself without my permission." In other words, if we are vulnerable to feeling threatened, others may use this to their advantage.

Third, *we may be unprepared to truly share our opinion.* Perhaps you have not thought through what you really feel about a particular situation. When others question you about your position, you realize the ground you stand on may have no firm foundation. You must do your homework and firm up your opinions. Use the opportunity to shore up your convictions so that you know what you know. Ask more questions and search out more facts so that you feel more secure with your opinions.

Finally, *find those with whom you can share your opinions for validation.* All of us need champions. Find friends who will consider your ideas. Ask them to critique your point of view to see if it can stand up to challenge. They may help you see some faults in your position and identify areas that need further work.

Deidre was an accomplished employee. She worked with other competent professionals and had always considered herself to be very effective in her job. But the insidious assault on her self-esteem at home, through Tom's consistent criticism of her opinions, combined with a residue of issues from her past, made her feel as if she were faltering on the job as well. Her usual confidence gave way to doubts and insecurities. She needed support and extra affirmation to bolster her flagging confidence.

Deidre and I agreed that our first task, as is always the case, was to make an accurate diagnosis. What exactly was going on? Together we determined that she had some old family issues that were being played out again with Tom. We determined that Tom had some need to be superior to her and others and used this power to undermine her self-confidence. Through counseling, prayer, and journaling, we began to seek ways to strengthen her inner convictions, assigning appropriate responsibility to herself and to Tom. We prepared the way for Tom to come in for counseling, which proved helpful in resolving many of their issues.

Abigail's Conviction

There are certainly many examples in Scripture about speaking with conviction. Perhaps none is as compelling as the story of Abigail, who saved her people from catastrophe during an encounter with David in 1 Samuel 25.

We read in this passage that Abigail was an intelligent and beautiful woman, but her rich husband, Nabal, was surly and mean. King David had sent some men to Nabal, reminding him that David and his men had protected Nabal's shepherds and flocks in the wilderness. Even though Nabal had considerable wealth, David's men did not take advantage of them. Now, David asks for some provisions as his men pass through Nabal's land.

But Nabal, whose name means "fool," greets King David's men with contempt. He insults them and offers them no food or drink. When the men tell David of their encounter with this nasty man, David is enraged. He vows to leave no man alive in Nabal's territory. He gathers his warriors and sets out to annihilate Nabal and his people.

One of the servants tells Abigail of the pending doom of her people. In this exciting story, we see a woman take the leadership role in her home because her husband had taken both her and David's men for granted. In spite of Nabal's shortcomings, Abigail was loyal to him and placed herself in danger to save him and their family. "Abigail lost no time. She took two hundred loaves of bread, two skins of wine, five dressed sheep, five seahs of roasted grain, a hundred cakes of raisins and two hundred cakes of pressed figs, and loaded them on donkeys" (25:18). Surely, as she was riding out to greet David, she was considering what she might say to a powerful man, armed, angry, and capable of destroying her family and friends.

What was going through her mind as she was preparing her speech? She must have been afraid. She was going to face King David and 400 seasoned warriors. She was essentially alone, except for a few of her servants, who had gone ahead. She must have considered her convictions: Even though Nabal was a fool, he did not deserve to die, she could protect her family with her wisdom, and perhaps she could avert disaster by assuaging David's rage.

When Abigail sees David, she gets off her donkey and bows to him. She asks that the blame fall on her head alone. She says what needs to be said with eloquence and conviction. She is clear, calm, concise, and speaks with conviction. David is moved and commends her by saying, "May you be blessed for your good judgment and for keeping me from bloodshed this day and from avenging myself with my own hands."

David accepts Abigail's gifts and sends her away in peace. She arrives home to find her drunken, irresponsible husband having a banquet. She waits until the following day to tell him what had happened. As soon as he heard the story, "his heart failed him and he became like a stone. About ten days later, the LORD struck Nabal and he died" (28:37-38).

Our story does not end here, however. David has not forgotten this woman's courage and convictions. Some time later, after learning of Nabal's death, David asks Abigail to become his wife—an honor befitting this courageous and heroic woman.

The Testing of Conviction

Before you engage your man in serious conversation about issues in your relationship, you need to ask yourself a few questions. Are you utterly committed to what you are saying? Do you really mean business? And are you really sure of what you want to say and why you want to say it?

Consider how prepared you are to answer the following questions:

- Do you have clarity in your thoughts about the particular issue?
- Do you feel compelled to follow through on this issue, even if doing so creates tension in your relationship?
- Do you know the foundation of your desires?

- Are you clear about what you must have as an outcome?

- Are you clear about scriptural principles that may bear upon your desires?

Our convictions are often not convictions at all until they have been tested. Often convictions come about through a process of developing a position on a particular issue, having it tested, and then finding it strengthened in the crucible of conflict. As others challenge our beliefs, those beliefs often become solidified.

Reflecting about the questions above may help you gain clarity and conviction about the issues in your life. They may help stabilize your thoughts and shore up the requests you make of your man.

The Risks of Conviction

Gaining clarity about inner convictions—knowing what you believe, why you believe it, and what it means to those around you—is not an easy or risk-free proposition. It takes work. It takes personal growth, which always means moving out of one's comfort zone and into the arena of risk.

What exactly are the risks of having and sharing personal convictions? What can this mean to your marriage? What may it mean to a person like Deidre?

It means taking the time to really know what you believe and why you believe it. Convictions do not come easily or cheaply. They do not fall into our lap like something falling out of the sky. We are not born with convictions. To be personal and strong, they are created and discovered in the fiery crucible of life. They will come from standing back and examining what you believe and why it is different from what your spouse may believe. When others would try to dissuade us from our convictions, we must take the time to carefully examine what we believe.

It means taking the risk of living our convictions. Obviously, having convictions is not enough. We must live them. We must believe them, own them, and then have the courage to live them out in our everyday lives. For Deidre, this meant determining how she truly felt about her husband traveling as much as he did, about the way he talked to her, and about her concerns about infidelity.

It means speaking our convictions to those around us. Convictions will almost always meet with resistance and disagreement. No one agrees with everything we say. If they do, our convictions are soft, vague, flimsy, and meaningless. When we take a stand, others will disagree. You can count on it. The real question is whether we can take the heat and tension involved when others don't like what we say or stand for.

It means that others will be forced to take us seriously. When we speak from our convictions, whether others agree or disagree with us, they will know where we stand. They will take us seriously. Unflinching, firm, supported with fact and not distortion, and resolute, we know what we know. We are secure in our beliefs but also willing to listen to new information.

It means that we have personal power. Standing on principles and biblical wisdom creates power. Power is not something nasty that is to be avoided. Used appropriately, it is a healthy thing. Our convictions, rooted in solid ground, let others know we cannot be trifled with. In fact, we are capable of influencing others. We can present information in such a way as to change people's minds.

The Benefits of Conviction

Certainly there are risks to having conviction. We can see this in the lives of Alexander, Gandhi, and Nancy Reagan. Those who dare to live by their convictions must pay a price. For some, the price is not cheap. Perhaps you can think of people you admire who hold strong beliefs and live them out in their lives. Most of the people who have garnered my admiration have been people of conviction—and they have paid a price for those convictions.

But as surely as convictions bring risks, they also bring benefits.

Convictions give meaning to our lives. As we reflect upon the life of Nancy Reagan and her ordeal over the past ten years, we immediately see the cost of her convictions. But she would undoubtedly be the first to say that her conviction to care for her dear Ronnie has been tremendously rewarding. It has given meaning to her life and to her husband's life. Conviction can give meaning to your life as well.

Convictions give direction to our lives. Our convictions propel us forward. Those things that are meaningful to us, those things that we must speak up about, will move us forward. They give us the energy to keep forging ahead regardless of obstacles. The apostle Paul tells us, "I press on to take hold of that for which Christ Jesus took hold of me....I do not consider myself yet to have taken hold of it. But one thing I do: Forgetting what is behind and straining toward what is ahead I press on toward the goal to win the prize for which God has called me heavenward in Christ Jesus" (Philippians 3:12-14).

Convictions give character to our lives. Who can look closely at Gandhi's life, or perhaps Mother Teresa's, and not be impressed by the character springing from conviction? The apostle Paul went through years of hardship and torture because of his overwhelming conviction of the love of Christ. Conviction can be just as powerful and moving in your life and mine.

Convictions influence others in our lives. Perhaps more germane to the purpose of this book, conviction influences others. Conviction can take your message and give it impetus. Grounded in solid thinking, scriptural integrity, and firm resolve, your convictions just might lead to changes in your man. Alexander may have been unable to dissuade his parents from moving, but we can be sure that they listened to his heartfelt emotions.

What Are Your Convictions?

And so we come to the hundred-dollar question: What are your convictions? What are you convinced that you must say to your man? What exactly are you sure you believe?

If you have trouble answering these questions, go back to the drawing board, sit alone with your journal, and reflect upon the things that have been burning in your heart for some time. What are these issues and how do you really feel about them?

Perhaps you will be surprised to hear that many women I talk to are not sure what they really and truly believe. When faced with the challenge of defending their beliefs, they falter. They are not as certain as they had thought about why they believe what they believe. They are not entirely positive about what they want from their man.

Just as surely as Abigail had to weigh the risks of presenting her petition to King David, Deirdre had to collect her thoughts and decide what she must say to Tom. She had to listen carefully to her heart, through reflection and prayer, and determine what to say to him. She had to remove the dross from the silver, finding the purest, most convicting issue to share with him. This homework prepared her to share her concerns in forthright manner, leading to changes that helped strengthen their marriage. Tom began to take her seriously, and together they created a stronger relationship based upon trust.

Perhaps this is where you are today. Perhaps you have been approaching your man without any real convictions. Perhaps you have had some gusto, only to be shot down when he confronted your reasoning. You may be frustrated, angry, and greatly perturbed. This will not change until you have shored up your convictions—when you reach the point of knowing what you know.

As you reflect upon what you believe and what you want to say to your man, the apostle James has something to say to us. He offers us a challenge.

> If any of you lacks wisdom, he should ask God, who gives generously to all without finding fault, and it will be given to him. But when he asks, he must believe and not doubt, because he who doubts is like a wave of the sea, blown and tossed by the wind. That man should not think he will receive anything from the Lord; he is a double-minded man, unstable in all he does (James 1:5-8).

Now we come to the last of our powerful Seven Cs—conciliation. Let's learn how to say what needs to be said with a heart of goodwill.

TEN

Saying It
with Conciliation

*I no longer consider myself the center of
the universe. I show up. I listen. I try to laugh.*

ANNA QUINDLEN

⚘ ✿ ⚘

People called her "Galloping Gertie." From her name, you would think she was a thoroughbred coming off a dominating win at the Preakness. Or perhaps a dark horse that had pulled out a come-from-behind win at the Kentucky Derby. Or maybe she was someone's loyal sidekick in an old Western movie.

Actually, Gertie was none of these. She, or rather it, was the Tacoma Narrows Bridge.

This 5939-foot-long structure, which had been needed for years, was designed to link two disparate worlds—Tacoma and Gig Harbor, Washington. For decades, people had talked about building a bridge that would connect the metropolitan cities of Tacoma and Seattle with rural Gig Harbor and the Olympic Peninsula. Without the bridge, folks had to rely on a slow, old ferry, or worse, drive miles around the Kitsap Peninsula to the other side. Two worlds were reaching for one another across a turbulent span of water.

With the vision secure and excitement high, a bright engineer was selected to design the structure. The green light was given for construction to begin on September 27, 1938. After more than a year and a half of backbreaking labor, the bridge opened to traffic on July 1, 1940.

But the bridge had problems. It was suspended by plate girders that caught the wind, rather than allowing it to pass through. As you might have guessed, this was a critical engineering *faux pas*. Just four months after it opened, during a major storm, Gertie began rolling and corkscrewing violently. Finally, it collapsed. Because it bucked like a bronco in a beehive, the bridge has been forever remembered as "Galloping Gertie."

Significant warning signs pointed to the bridge's collapse. Minor oscillations continued for weeks, and engineers made various unsuccessful efforts to control the movement. Ironically, people were drawn to the "galloping" bridge. They lined up to experience the sensation of crossing the rolling center span. Cars crossed the dangerous bridge, disappearing into concrete gullies and then reappearing as the bridge rose and fell. Finally, however, the structure could not withstand the vicious winds that whipped through the Narrows between Tacoma and Gig Harbor.

Reporter Leonard Coatsworth witnessed the collapse.

> Just as I drove past the towers, the bridge began to sway violently from side to side. Before I realized it, the tilt became so violent that I lost control of the car....I jammed on the brakes and got out, only to be thrown onto my face against the curb. Around me I could hear concrete cracking. I started to get my dog, Tubby, but was thrown again before I could reach my car. The car itself began to slide from side to side of the roadway. On hand and knees most of the time, I crawled 500 yards or more to the towers....My breath was coming in gasps; my knees were raw and bleeding, my hands bruised and swollen from gripping the concrete curb....Toward

the last, I risked rising to my feet and running a few
yards at a time....Safely back at the toll plaza, I saw
the bridge in its final collapse and saw my car plunge
into the Narrows.[1]

Galloping Gertie is now part of Tacoma history—and urban
legend. For years, a rumor floated around that the designer had
embezzled monies intended for the bridge, leading to a compro-
mised structure. It was never proven. What is certain is that for
ten more years, Tacoma and the Olympic Mountains recre-
ational area remained unconnected. People in Tacoma had to
travel the long way by road if they wanted to get to the coast.
Eventually, ingenuity and tenacity prevailed, and a new bridge
was constructed.

Wherever people find an opportunity to link two worlds,
they seem to find a way to do it. We are forever reaching,
stretching, trying to forge new relationships.

Bridges are vital to our commerce and lifestyle. Much like effective communication, those that are properly constructed
link worlds together. In relationships, we build bridges by
speaking with conciliation.

If you have struggled in your marriage, you may feel like the
bridge linking you to your spouse has collapsed. You may feel a
bit like the reporter who watched his car and beloved pet fall
hundreds of feet into the swirling waters below. You may feel as
if you have been stranded on a defective bridge that sways dangerously and unpredictably. You may feel as if you are hanging
on for dear life.

In this chapter, we will explore another C that can improve
the bond between partners. This powerful C is conciliation—that
disarming, calming tool that can bring separate worlds together.

A Sinister Tension

Most troubled relationships do not collapse suddenly. Two
worlds do not normally separate in one windswept, catastrophic

action. The demise of a relationship is a slow, insidious process. An ongoing current of hurt and anger, like persistent water, can gradually erode the landscape of a marriage.

Early in your relationship, you probably felt the emotional elevation that comes with falling in love. Psychopharmacologists have documented the high that lovers experience—the natural hormones and chemicals that course through our bodies, creating an overwhelming sense of well-being. Dr. Michael R. Liebowitz, associate professor of clinical psychiatry at Columbia University, suggests, "The mystical experience of oneness that lovers undergo may be caused by an increase in the production of the neurotransmitter serotonin."[2]

Lovers cling to the illusion of romance because being in love feels so wonderful. If someone could bottle the experience and sell it, he would be a millionaire many times over. But, alas, the illusion fades. Slowly for most, more rapidly for some, tension enters the relationship. Where once you saw a shining knight on a white steed, you now see a rumpled, unshaven man astride a donkey. Tension and conflict have dashed your dreams.

A little stress is tolerable. A faded dream is not as bad as a nightmare. The shining knight can still be seen here and there.

A healthy marriage can endure and even thrive under these conditions. Most partners recognize that conflict is an inevitable part of a relationship. It follows us wherever we go, so we really cannot continue blaming others for our troubles. The fact is, every area of life where conflict is present has one common denominator: us.

And so we must learn to cope with conflict. We must learn to manage it and not let it manage us.

Polarized Couples

But what do we do if the chasm between our spouse and us is too great? What if too little of the bridge remains that connects us to our mate? What if tension has grown beyond reasonable limits? What if you have been trying, without success, to make contact with him for some time but find the ravine nearly impossible to navigate?

Let's review how our book began. We visited with Adam, Eve, and God in the Garden of Eden. You recall that Adam and Eve disobeyed God; Eve ate the forbidden fruit, and sin entered the world. Harmony and bliss with God was stained with enmity. Man against man; man against woman. Conflict became a part of our everyday lives.

Conflict, like a collapsed bridge, often creates separation between parties. Unhealthy conflict is often the reason for ruined relationships and marriages. Although we do not know exactly what went on between Adam and Eve after the Fall, I believe that pride and dissension became a central part of their lives.

Consider the anatomy of conflict and its typical parts.

First, *conflict begins with a desire.* We want something from our partner. We want them to behave differently. Perhaps we don't like the way they are treating us. Perhaps we don't like the fact that they are ignoring us. We have desires and needs, and these needs are sometimes not being met. Having desires is not a bad thing. In fact, our desires make us unique. These desires originate from our particular background, our beliefs, and our faith.

Second, *unmet needs and desires lead to resentment.* When this occurs, we rehearse how we are not getting what we think we deserve. We want something, believe we are entitled to it, and become resentful when our spouse doesn't deliver it.

Third, *conflict intensifies when we demand our way.* Conflict becomes more severe when we assume that we are right and insist on having things our way. A demanding person allows very little room for negotiation.

Demanding people are usually very rigid. They see things in black and white rather than shades of gray. Consequently, lines are drawn and couples are polarized.

Fourth, *conflict becomes entrenched when our point of view narrows.* When we are caught in the throes of extreme conflict, the narrowing of perspective intensifies. We defend our point of view and our right to have it. We may "camp" on the facts as we see them, failing to acknowledge the validity of the other person's perspective.

Fifth, *we judge the other person's point of view.* We may criticize and dismiss any opinion that differs from our own. Failing to acknowledge that viewpoints are rarely simply "right or wrong," we back others and ourselves into corners with our harsh judgments.

Finally, *we try to coerce others into agreeing with our point of view.* Either subtly or overtly, when others disagree with us on important matters, we may attempt to make them "see the light." We have desires, we demand our way, and we ultimately try to make others conform to our values and expectations. This may take the form of heated arguments or the softer form of coercion: pouting. It may also take the form of angry outbursts or silent withdrawals.

Either way, we want the other person to change and are not interested in moving from our entrenched position.

A Matter of Preferences

In my counseling, I often meet with couples who are attempting to repair broken bridges that have created distance in their relationship. Ginger and Daniel came to see me because they felt alienated from one another. They had been married for seven years and were severely conflicted over whether or not to homeschool their young children.

Ginger was a 33-year-old woman who had deliberately chosen to be a homemaker. College educated, she had shortened her career as a teacher to stay home with her children, an agreement she and Daniel had made early in their relationship. Modestly dressed with long brown hair, her unhappiness had taken a toll on her health. She suffered from stress and sleep disorders. She had been struggling with debilitating anxiety for several months, and her physician recommended that she and her husband seek counseling.

Daniel was 32. He dressed casually in slacks and a sport shirt. But nothing was casual about his demeanor. He worked as a technical analyst for a major corporation. He too was plagued by tension and unhappy with their marriage. At our first session, he stated that he was reluctantly willing to participate in counseling.

"So, what has brought you two in today?" I asked at their first appointment.

Ginger spoke right up.

"I'm a nervous wreck. We fight constantly over things that are ridiculous—where to tune up the car, how much to keep in our checking account, what stores to shop at. But most important is that I stay home with the kids and think they should be homeschooled. The schools around here are horrible, and I don't want our kids subjected to the profanity and violence in the schools. But Daniel doesn't agree with me, and we fight about it all the time. This argument has become so big that it has boiled over into everything from who takes the kids to soccer practice to how a dish towel is supposed to be hung on the refrigerator door."

Daniel jumped in. "I've studied the issue and believe the kids will get a better education in the public schools. Studies show that kids have a broader range of learning experiences in public schools. It's really a big deal to me, and I don't want to see my kids turn into wimps by being homeschooled."

"How can you say that?" Ginger replied. "I have no intention of turning them into wimps. The kids will be just fine. I'm a teacher, after all, and I know how to raise our kids so that they get the education they need."

"So if you are a teacher, you know that kids from home-schools don't have all the opportunities that kids in public schools get. You can't possibly argue that."

Daniel and Ginger stared at one another. Both were angry. Both had taken a position and were defending it vigorously.

"So, do you two go round and round about this issue at home?"

Both nodded.

"I'm not going to keep fighting about it," Ginger said. "I am not letting my little boys go to public school. That place is evil as far as I'm concerned. They're not going and that's it!"

"And that is exactly the kind of attitude that infuriates me," countered Daniel. "She knows what's right, and I'm supposed to cave in and do everything her way. I went to our associate pastor and he agreed with me. He told me nothing is wrong with the public schools."

It is not unusual for couples to disagree passionately about issues. In fact, most of us have strong feelings about certain things and are willing to fight for what we think is right. So, what is the problem with Daniel and Ginger, you might ask? Why are they stuck?

The problem is this:

- This kind of fighting doesn't work, plain and simple. Ginger and Daniel are butting heads with little regard for each other's feelings. If this behavior continues, it could ruin their marriage.

- This kind of fighting goes against fair fighting rules, which emphasize each person's right to think what they think and feel what they feel.

- This kind of fighting goes against Scripture, which encourages us to think of others more highly than ourselves and to guard against selfish desires (Romans 12:3; James 1:13-15).

- This kind of fighting does not move people closer together. It is not conciliatory. Rather, it creates distance and hostility.

How did I counsel this couple? I pointed out several things to Daniel and Ginger, and then I stood back and hoped they would make a shift in their thinking and actions.

Specifically, I focused on the following points:

- Their bickering was obviously not settling the dispute or bringing them closer to one another.
- Neither of them was right or wrong.
- This issue was a matter of preferences.
- They could learn to negotiate a win-win solution that created a bridge to one another.
- They needed to display tenderness toward one another rather than maintaining judgmental attitudes.
- Creating a bridge would make both of them feel better and would honor God.

In recent years, I have grappled with the fact that I have been a lot like Ginger and Daniel. While I prided myself in my ability to negotiate and see various sides of a matter, I too often saw things as right and wrong when they were matters of preference. My pride and self-righteousness stopped me from looking deeply into myself for the longest time. But eventually, I looked more closely.

What I found did not make me feel very good about myself. Deep down, I really wanted my way and found the means, often subtle, to get it. Down deep, I was very judgmental; I believed that my way was right and best.

My new insight did not come without diligent thought and a significant amount of pain. I eventually realized how demanding I can be and how much havoc my demands place upon my primary relationships.

Recently, a colleague wanted to implement a formal, written policy for new employees at the office. He had done his homework and pointed out that "we really should have these kinds of policies in place." I bristled at the thought of adding this work to my schedule. I began to point out that this policy manual would be nice but was unnecessary. I watched how I interacted with him, forced myself to really listen to his point of view, and acknowledged the importance of this manual to him. I had to work against my natural desire to criticize his thinking and position before I could begin to work with him.

Perhaps you can relate with Ginger, Daniel, and myself. Perhaps you are coming to see the role you play in ongoing conflict. You may be acting the part of the innocent bystander, but the velvet hammer you wield is just as deadly as if it were steel.

The Heart of the Matter

What exactly do I mean when I talk about conciliation? And how can we speak with conciliation, especially when we feel we are the victim of some wrongdoing? Doesn't this fly in the face of what we have been saying so far in this book? Actually not.

Conciliation has to do with motives. It has to do with the "why" behind what you are saying. Your purpose, when speaking with conciliation, is to appease and assuage your spouse. You want to make peace, not war. You want to create harmony, not animosity. You want to work cooperatively, not competitively. You want to build a bridge, not destroy it.

Some of you may be saying, "Just a minute. I thought that I was learning these techniques so that I could influence my spouse. I thought the tools in this book were designed to get my partner to listen to me and then do what I wanted."

Well, that is partly correct. I do want your spouse to listen to you. That is critically important. But we are looking for a win-win solution, not a win-lose proposition. The problem is that if you score an overwhelming victory, you actually lose. In the world of relating, winning over someone can create even more conflict and resentment. That leads to greater distance between partners.

So, as you approach this chapter, I ask you to examine your motives and consider the following questions:

- Why are you saying what you are saying?
- Why are you asking for what you want?
- What are your real motives?
- Do you have the need to be right?
- Do your desires stem from selfishness?
- Are you intent on manipulating and outmaneuvering your spouse?
- Are you motivated to use fancy words so that you can talk him into, or out of, something?

Hopefully, your motivation is to be heard and understood. Hopefully, you are motivated to build a bridge to him so that you can enjoy a relationship filled with peace and harmony.

When you set out on the journey of exploring your heart, you must be ready to do some serious soul-searching. A good Scripture to meditate upon in this matter is Philippians 2:2-4:

> Make my joy complete by being like-minded, having the same love, being one in spirit and purpose. Do nothing out of selfish ambition or vain conceit, but in humility consider others better than yourselves. Each of you should look not only to your own interests, but also to the interests of others.

Here we see the apostle Paul instructing on the importance of being like-minded, of being one in spirit and purpose. He warns against selfish ambition, that drive to sneak and manipulate, to twist facts in an attempt to outmaneuver our opponent. Then he hits the nail on the head by emphasizing the importance of humility, which will encourage us to consider both our own and others' interests. There's the bridge! If we are concerned about our mate's interests as well as our own, we will always be in the business of building bridges.

In one of His longest recorded sermons, the Sermon on the Mount, Christ offers another perspective on the matter.

> Why do you look at the speck of sawdust in your brother's eye and pay no attention to the plank in your own eye? How can you say to your brother, "Let me take the speck out of your eye" when all the time there is a plank in your own eye? You hypocrite, first take the plank out of your own eye, and then you will see clearly to remove the speck from your brother's eye (Matthew 7:3-5).

This passage is often subtitled "Judging Others." However, it is also about looking into your own heart and taking care of your own business before confronting your mate about his. It is about not being so presumptuous as to think you are capable of seeing your husband's difficulties when blinded by your own problems. Our issues blind us to seeing others' conflicts clearly. We must do our own work before we can even think about talking to others about their problems. Then, after having worked on our issues, after examining our part in the matter, we have a changed heart that can be helpful to others.

I recall an incident not long ago when my friend Dean approached me, presumably for the purpose of reconciling differences between us. We'd had a heated disagreement weeks earlier that left distance between us. We both knew that we would have to talk again to resolve the problem, but I was still too annoyed to approach him.

One Sunday, he came up to me after church. My heart quickened. I hoped that he would apologize for his part in our conflict and create an opportunity for me to apologize as well.

I was unprepared for what happened. The gist of the conversation is as follows:

"David, I need to tell you that I think you have something going on in your life that made you talk to me in anger a few weeks ago. Maybe it's something in your personal life or something going on at work. I know you've had some problems lately. The Lord has told me that I had nothing to do with our argument, but I am ready to talk again when you can apologize for what you did wrong. I think you were overly harsh with me, and that was wrong."

Needless to say, I was speechless. Here was a friend who had the audacity to put the entire blame on me and none on himself. He acknowledged the gulf between us, handed me the pick and shovel, and put me in charge of building the bridge back to him. This was not the hand of conciliation but the hand of judgment. I walked away wounded, fuming with anger. The gulf between us had widened.

I have had some time to think about this event. I realize I cannot be too critical of Dean, for he is every man (including me) and every woman. Christ warned against this kind of behavior. He told us that people would point out the speck in another's eye rather than go to the optometrist to remove the detritus that impairs their own sight. Certainly, while annoyed, I could understand Dean's actions.

Dean and I talked later. I shared my hurt, my anger, and my desire for him to take at least some of the responsibility for our differences. He did, and he was more amenable to reconciliation. He took time to think about our disagreement and wanted to rekindle our friendship.

The Work of Conciliation

Conciliation is not easy work. In fact, it is humbling work because speaking with conciliation means that we will approach our partner ready to do several critical things.

First, *we will be ready to acknowledge the desires in our hearts that cause problems.* The Bible tells us that conflict arises from the desires that do battle in our hearts (James 4:1-3; Matthew 15:18-19). We must wage war with our own heart before we can confront our mate. We must do battle with the desires we have to subdue—especially the desire to come out "one up" against our mate. We must root out the sneaky desires that drive us to manipulate the situation for our own gain.

Second, *we must be prepared to face our own idolatry.* Anytime we are excessively preoccupied with something, believing that it will satisfy all of our needs, we have created an idol. This will lead to conflict with God and must be dealt with. Be careful if you are obsessing about someone's "wrongs." See if this obsession has taken the foremost position in your mind, a place that must be reserved for your relationship with God.

Third, *we must take care of the log in our own eye before we can talk about the speck in our mate's eye.* Have you prayed for wisdom and insight into your part in the problem? Having done our own work, having acknowledged the hurt that we have caused by our actions, we come humbly to our partner about their "speck" that may need attention. You can imagine the bridge-building possibilities that will occur when we begin with this kind of attitude.

Finally, *we will see clearly enough to talk to our mate about his speck.* Now, having listed our wrongs and apologized, we have completed our heart surgery and are ready to talk about our feelings about his behavior. Having changed our attitude and shown that we are ready to walk the walk and not just talk the talk, we stand before him with real credibility.

These steps prepare the way for restoring the relationship. Matthew 18 gives further instruction that may be helpful as you consider approaching your spouse with issues that need to be addressed. Matthew 18 is an important piece of the puzzle when handling conflict in a marriage or any other relationship. Let's look at what this Scripture can teach us.

> If your brother sins against you, go and show him his
> fault, just between the two of you. If he listens to you,
> you have won your brother over. But if he will not
> listen, take one or two others along, so that "every
> matter may be established by the testimony of two or
> three witnesses" (Matthew 18:15-16).

At first glance, this passage appears to be saying that we should go to others who have wronged us and set them straight. However, the verses preceding and following this text show that the heart of God is one of restoration, not condemnation. Just before this passage we read about the loving shepherd who seeks out the lost sheep and rejoices when it is found. Just after this passage are verses reminding us that we must be merciful and forgiving to others.

Our attitude when approaching our mate about a sensitive matter must include honesty and gentleness, not anger. Our approach certainly must address how he has contributed to the conflict, but we come to the table with a spirit of restoration, not judgment.

Daniel and Ginger were able to make great progress in their relationship when they saw that what they were doing would ultimately erode their love for one another and destroy their family. More importantly, they were able to recognize their own selfish ambitions in trying to change the other's mind. With hard work, they slowly let loose of their grip on their position and listened to their partner.

They were able to find a solution that worked for both of them. They agreed to homeschool their children, but they would work with other homeschoolers to provide the social interaction Daniel wanted for the kids. Daniel and Ginger came to understand and appreciate each other's point of view and right to have it. They built a strong, functional bridge to one another through conciliation.

Pray for Humility, Wisdom, and Gentleness

The message of this book is that we must be willing to talk about thorny issues. We must be willing to confront behavior that is destroying relationships. Our approach to these conversations is critical.

In *The Book of Love,* Daphne Rose Kingma reminds us that gentleness is an essential ingredient on the road to conciliation.

> Gentleness is the soft virtue, the cloudy featheriness of spirit that allows you to move toward the person you love, and through each circumstance you face, in an easy, graceful, and gracious manner—touching delicately, listening openly, feeling with empathy, seeing with eyes of compassion. Gentleness eases the way, adds refinement and grace to the journey, softens the blows, cushions the sorrows, lightens the burdens.[3]

Can you imagine entering each discussion with your spouse with an attitude of gentleness, regardless of the emotion and severity of the topic? Can you imagine how this attitude of conciliation would help you approach your partner? Can you imagine how this would make clear your desire to build a connection that could lead to an equitable resolution?

As you ready yourself to talk to your spouse in new and powerful ways, add to your list the technique of speaking with conciliation. These steps will help you prepare yourself:

- Pray for humility and wisdom.
- Understand your own weaknesses and how you have contributed to the problem.
- Remove the plank from your eye.
- See your partner as complex, loving, and concerned about doing the best he can do for today.
- Choose an appropriate time and place to talk.

- Listen carefully and seek to understand him.
- Speak to build up rather than tear down.
- Demonstrate respect by showing genuine concern.
- Allow for differences.
- Do your part and leave the rest to God.

Although relationships carry no guarantees, if you approach your mate with these attitudes and behaviors, growth is likely to take place. What is certain, however, is that you will be changed in the process—for the better. Your heart will be softened, your vision broadened, your faith challenged and deepened.

Having learned The Seven Cs, we will now focus on practical approaches that combine several of these strategies. In our next chapter, we will explore how courage, in combination with a willingness to exert consequences with the expectation of change, can be an incredibly powerful tool.

Eleven

Saying It with Courage

Your passion is your power.

LAURIE BETH JONES

Sandy was a plain girl. Her unmanageable brown hair hung over her eyes, and the collar of the too-small, hand-me-down blouse she'd been wearing for several days in a row—the source of much ridicule from other kids—was badly stained. She had two pairs of jeans she wore regularly, though both were too large for her. When she timidly asked her grandmother if she could have some new clothes, her grandmother scolded her and told her that she didn't have enough money for frivolous things. It took all she had to raise Sandy and her older sister.

As if being poor and plain were not enough, Sandy also felt terribly lonely. At eight years old, she and her ten-year-old sister wondered when they might see their mother again. Sandy's grandmother would only say that her mother had "problems with the law," which was why she could only come to see Sandy and her sister every once in a while. What she had done to end up in jail was a dark secret Sandy's grandmother never talked about. When Sandy was very young, she wondered if her mother had killed someone or robbed a bank. But she never asked, and her grandmother never told. She still did not know the truth of the matter.

Once, Sandy had screwed up her courage to ask her grandmother about her father, whom she had never seen or known. She received only vague information—"He had to live away"—leaving Sandy to fill in the blanks. Sandy decided her father must be in jail with her mother, though she didn't find out until four years later that her father had simply decided not to be involved with his children. He had apparently never married their mother and had abandoned the three of them early when the children were very young.

Other than her mother and grandmother, Sandy's older sister, Susan, was her only family, and she guarded that relationship fiercely. Even though her sister was often mean to her, Sandy always forgave her and did favors to gain her affection. She would often share her favorite toys with her and even do some of her chores for her. It was too painful to have Susan mad at her, especially when Sandy didn't know when she would see her mother again.

Even though Sandy knew that her mother had legal problems, she felt guilty about being abandoned. She imagined that if she had been pretty or smart, her mother would not have left her and Susan. Try as she might, she could not get rid of the nagging guilt that increasingly dominated her personality.

Sandy's grandmother, with whom they had lived most of their life, had a volatile temperament. The days when she was kind and loving were special days in their home. "Granny" would sit down with the girls and read to them or play board games like Scrabble. But in an instant, her mood would change, and she would spew anger about being responsible for raising two young children. She would tell them to play in their rooms and to make sure they were quiet. Sandy learned to watch Granny's moods, knowing when she could be playful and when she should be silent.

Sandy wondered about Granny too. Where had Grandpa gone? She had a vague memory of him, but he too had disappeared when she was small. Why did Granny live alone? Why was she so sad so often? Was it something she and Susan had done? Sandy thought about these questions at night when she lay quietly in her bed.

Sandy's mother never did come home to stay. Sandy never learned what had happened to her grandfather, except that he walked out one day and never came back. She never discovered how to make her grandmother happy, though she never gave up trying. She spent a lot of energy doing her chores, helping out in the kitchen, and trying to be "a good girl."

While Sandy's older sister escaped the pain of their home life through early promiscuity and drug involvement, Sandy chose a different path. Her temperament could not handle the dangers that seemed so appealing to her sister. Sandy felt happy and safe when immersed in a Nancy Drew mystery novel. Just after the start of her eleventh grade year, however, she met a boy who made her tingle all over. Kyle was kind to her and wanted to know everything about her. No one had shown that much interest in her before. The romance blossomed, and she saw an opportunity to leave her grandmother's house. After several months Sandy dropped out of school and moved in with him. After about a year of living together and working at fast-food restaurants, she discovered she was pregnant. They were married a short time later.

Kyle was not kind and attentive for long. He liked to run the streets and drink. During his drunken binges, he became verbally and emotionally abusive. Sandy had no way to understand that her feeling of unworthiness led her to pick a boy who acted out his frustrations and aggressions on her. She put up with his behavior because it was strangely comfortable. No one had ever treated her special on a consistent basis. Why should she expect anything different now?

The years went by, but Sandy's issues were never resolved.

Facing 40, weighed down by years of anger and hurt, Sandy came to counseling for help with her third troubled marriage. She felt ashamed of her two failed relationships, yet there was a spark inside that kept pushing for something healthy. She had endured 15 years of marriage to her first husband, 15 years of his alcohol abuse and violence. She had struggled with a second marriage that lasted only three years, and now she was in the second year of her third marriage. She wanted something more, something better for herself. Her painful childhood, in combination with a young adult life of turmoil and her turbulent relationships with men, primed her to seek more from this marriage.

Sandy felt ashamed of her divorces, but she had a glimmer of hope and pride in her recent choices. She had developed a reasonable career as a medical transcriptionist in spite of her limited education. She shared with me how she had gone back to church after attending only briefly as a child. She shared how she wanted more from marriage and men and wanted help in learning how to set healthy boundaries for herself. She desperately wanted to avoid repeating the patterns that had made her so depressed for so many years.

Sandy was now married to a man she had fallen in love with a few years ago. She loved Kelly and wanted to save their marriage, but she had serious concerns:

"I think I truly fell in love for the first time when I met Kelly a few years ago. I don't think I've ever really been in love before. When I married Kyle, it was for security, not for love. I hate to admit it, but my second marriage was for money. This time was different. It was great. It still is great in some ways, but I put up with too much. Kelly is a good man and treats me well. I am beginning to demand respect. But he is so selfish. He doesn't really think about me as an equal partner. He spends money any way he wants and doesn't think there is anything wrong with it. He has so many toys and puts us into debt without any worries about it. I am the one who worries and stays awake at night wondering how we will pay the bills. I am the one who finds ways to extend our credit to pay the bills. And he lets me. If I try to talk about these problems with him, he gets mad, and I hate that."

Sandy and I met for some time, talking about her painful childhood and the scars left from the abandonment by her mother, father, and, to a certain extent, her grandmother. Sandy wonders if she has the right to ask for more in her marriage. But gradually, over the years, Sandy has gained more strength than she knows. With newfound courage, she is prepared to seek more in her marriage with Kelly. With a strength forged of hardship, she is ready to talk to her husband in new ways.

Galileo Galilei

You need courage to change—and not to change. As you consider what you want to say to your man and how you want to say it, you need to understand that your message will not be communicated effectively unless it rides on the shoulders of another critical trait—courage. Sandy has it, and so do you. So did Galileo Galilei.

Galileo was a man who wrestled with his convictions and his community, trying to decide if he should give in to the pressures around him or hold to his convictions. He had to decide what he would say to his superiors when his discoveries went against popular opinion.

Born in Pisa, Italy, to Vincenzo Galilei and Guilia Ammannati, his father was a music teacher and a fine lute player. Galileo was their first child, and they decided that he would become a medical doctor. Galileo, however, had other plans. He was fascinated with mathematics and soon learned to apply these skills to the study of the heavens. The rest, as they say, is history. By the age of 25, he was a professor of mathematics at the University of Pisa. It was there, in the campanile, the famous leaning tower, that he conducted his revolutionary experiments, showing that heavier and lighter objects both fall to the ground at the same speed, shattering old theories.

He later used his mathematical skills to make telescopes and study astronomy. Using a telescope he had designed himself, he was the first to recognize that the Milky Way consisted of millions of stars, and he is credited with discovering the moons of Jupiter in 1610. In a very short time, Galileo made more discoveries than had been made for many years. However, one discovery created a great deal of trouble between him and the Catholic Church.

Through rigorous experiments, Galileo confirmed the Copernican theory that the earth was not the center of the universe. This was heresy, according to the Church, which strongly believed in a geocentric universe. Galileo was left with a most difficult decision—follow his conscience and face the Inquisition, or recant his beliefs. He was threatened with torture unless he withdrew his opinions, and subsequently he did recant them. However, when he courageously decided to pursue his interests and theories, he was placed under house arrest for the rest of his life.

Galileo was unable or unwilling to let his passions die. He faced ridicule, shame, and public censure, but he still held to his beliefs. Faced with the prospect of torture and possible death, he secretly pursued and promoted his studies. He kept detailed journals, later published, that provided important new information. That is courage. He said what needed to be said, he said it courageously, and we benefited from it. In the twentieth century, the Catholic Church decided that he had committed no sin or heresy.

Markings of Courage

Perhaps your life is neither as dramatic as Sandy's nor as dynamic and brilliant as Galileo's. Perhaps your life is filled with simple things, strung together from day to day to form an ordinary life. Even if that is the case, I suspect that upon closer inspection we would find that your life has the markings of courage. We would also discover that courage is necessary if you are to move toward saying it so your man will listen. Let's consider exactly what comprises courage.

First, *courageous people see things the way they really are.* Have you noticed that courageous people do not blink in the face of adversity? They are willing to acknowledge problems and begin to make necessary changes. Scott Peck, in his seminal work *The Road Less Traveled,* says that the essential ingredients of mental health include the ability to face life the way it is and then decide how to move forward. Courageous people do not wear rose-colored glasses when facing life's pain; they see things clearly.

Second, *courageous people accept life the way it is.* This does not mean that they do not try to change things. It means that they are willing to see things for what they are, accept that framework for reality, and make decisions based upon that information.

Sandy gradually faced the facts that were haunting her—particularly her abandonment by her mother and father and her grandmother's emotional volatility. She quit trying to make excuses for them and came to acknowledge this as part of the fabric of her life. She slowly accepted the fact that she had made many poor choices in response to her early neglect, causing her great pain, and now she wanted to make healthier decisions.

Third, *courageous people take risks.* Sometimes the risk involves public humiliation—or worse, as was the case for Galileo. Sometimes it involves loss of admiration or affection, as it did for Sandy. Sometimes it means that we will risk our safety and security for a time.

Lance Armstrong, the famous repeat winner of the Tour de France, is certainly a brave man in our culture today. Our respect for him was forever sealed when he courageously fought cancer, defeated it, and went on to win the Tour de France—six times in a row!

Fourth, *courageous people follow their passions.* We can see this in the lives of Sandy, Galileo, and Armstrong. These people, in their own way, listened to their hearts and pursued their goals. Their passions provided the "juice" to move forward against difficulties. They provided the impetus to climb mountains, face scrutiny, and generally go against the grain.

Fifth, *courageous people follow their passions through adversity.* We know that adversity often makes us stronger. We may wish for a shorter path to inner strength and confidence, but the path usually winds its way through the trials and struggles of life. If we are to reach our destination, we must traverse this path.

Hindsight is a wonderful thing. We often see things much more clearly through the rearview mirror. I still remember being fired from my first job as a young man. I was devastated. I had worked hard for years at a local restaurant, first as a busboy and then a cook. I took pride in my work. I was taking some college classes at the time as well and hoped that the restaurant job would see me through my early college years.

One day, however, new management came in, decided that I was not part of their A team, and gave me my walking papers. Bitter and angry, I was very discouraged, not to mention frightened about how I would pay for school. But, as our parents wisely say, "Things have a way of working out." Or, as the Scriptures say, "In all things God works for the good of those who love him" (Romans 8:28).

As you might have guessed, my adversity gave me the impetus to forge ahead more forcefully with my schooling, which turned out to be an excellent move. I was able to find a field of study that was richly rewarding for me, and I have been with it for the past 28 years. Who knows where I might be today had I been given a promotion at the restaurant instead of being shown the door.

Finally, *courageous people believe in themselves and in God's plan.* We see this point repeated many times in the Scriptures. The stories have the same essential parts: protagonist, mission, obstacle, victory. It may not always be the victory we want or hope for, but even tragedy is ultimately redeemed in one way or another. Courageous people have a way of seeing beyond the obstacles that show up on their path. They have a way of utilizing creative problem solving and emerging the victor. They know that God has brought them through trials in the past and that He will do so again.

A Matter of Heart

Something is very appealing about courageous people. We stand back and watch Rosa Parks dare to stand up against overwhelming cultural norms, refusing to move to the back of the bus. We stand in awe as teacher Christa McAuliffe represents every working man and woman by training to become an astronaut, only to meet a premature death.

We hold these women in high regard and perhaps even exaggerate their abilities and courage. We tell ourselves that they are extraordinary, that we could never access such superhuman abilities. They are a breed apart. But when we think this way we dilute our own capabilities. We minimize what God can and will do in the lives of ordinary people like ourselves.

David Whyte, in his book *Crossing the Unknown Sea*, dismisses the distinction between ordinary and extraordinary courage.

> We say to ourselves that we need more than ordinary courage, but really there is no ordinary courage. Either we are courageous or we are not. But the key is in the word *courage* itself. The word *courage* arises from the French *coeur,* meaning heart. To be courageous means at the bottom to be heartfelt. To begin with we take only those steps which we can do in a

heartfelt fashion, and then slowly increase our
stride as we become familiar with the direct connection between our passion and our courage. Without
some kind of fire in our conversation...life becomes
just another game plan.[1]

And so, to all of the techniques and tools you have discovered thus far in this book, you must now add *heart*. You must
listen to the deep part of yourself, the culmination of aches and
pains, joys and sorrows, that makes you the unique person you
have become. I ask you to access the core part of your being,
where spirit meets Spirit, where *heart* resides, and let it guide
and *encourage* you.

Jesus knew the power of *heart*. Sensing His disciples' discouragement at His announcement that He would not be with
them much longer, He says in John 14:1, "Do not let your
hearts be troubled. Trust in God; trust also in me." He recognized the heart as the seat of our emotions, but also as a place
of courage. He goes on to say, "I am going there to prepare a
place for you. And if I go and prepare a place for you, I will come
back and take you to be with me that you may also be where I
am." In essence, He is saying, "Take *heart*. Be encouraged."

Mary's Courage

Mary is a teenager when we meet her. She is young, poor,
unmarried, and pregnant. She is confused, lonely, and frightened. This brings a certain image to mind, one that does not
seem to fit the picture of someone who will escort our Savior
into the world.

This simple girl is "greatly troubled" at hearing about her role
in the birth of the Savior. Who wouldn't be frightened at the
prospect of being pregnant as a virgin? Yet we read that she is
in a "humble state." This creates an even more dramatic
scene—a plain, young woman, chosen apparently because of her
heart and not because of her standing in society. She is chosen

because of her courage, not because of her ability. Listen to her words:

"My soul glorifies the Lord, and my spirit rejoices in God my Savior. For he has been mindful of the humble state of his servant. From now on, all generations will call me blessed" (Luke 1:48).

Although we do not know much about this girl, we can be sure of one thing: She is courageous. She faced adversity and overcame it. She persevered under what must have been grueling circumstances, probably including public ridicule, ostracism, and shame. Buoyed by her mission, she showed a self-confidence and a confidence in God beyond her years.

We can learn many lessons from Mary, and one of them is that we must not discount ourselves as potential vessels for God's will and way. If God can use a poor, naive teenager, disgraced in the eyes of a skeptical world, He can surely use you and me. He can take our simplicity and make more of it, He can take our limits and create abundance, He can knead courage into the cracks and crevices of our lives where fear once hid.

The gospel message rings out again and again: You don't need eloquence, fame, or fortune to bring hope to a dying world. You don't need those qualities to bring a new message to your man. All you need is a dash of courage to send an important message to a man who needs to listen. You need what this poor young woman had—a mission, a message, and the courage to deliver it.

Expecting Change

We practice the techniques discussed in this book for a reason. We have a purpose and a mission. Yes, it is in part just so that we can be heard. And, of course, it is also so that we will be taken seriously and understood.

But this is not enough. To be heard, to be taken seriously, and to be understood are vitally important. But you want even more than that. You want change as well. Your life and marriage have a higher calling, and living in mediocrity does not suffice.

Many people might tell you to settle for less, but I challenge you to raise the bar of expectations instead of lowering it. If you expect that "this is as good as it gets," it surely will be. You must dream large and anticipate that change will occur.

Envision your man listening to what you need. Imagine him looking into your eyes, reflecting that he heard you, and acknowledging that you deserve change. Can you see it? It can happen, but you must first make it clear that you expect change. You are not willing to settle for half-measures. The health of your marriage is too important for you to settle for less than the best.

Now that you have practiced what you want to say and exactly how you want to say it, you are ready to add courage to your message. You are ready to make perfectly clear what you need to feel respected in this marriage.

Take a moment to answer the following questions to help make your expectations clear, knowing that clarity in your message increases the chances that your needs will be met.

- Exactly what do you want from your man?
- What is the old behavior that needs modification?
- What does the new behavior look like?
- How will you know when the desired change has occurred?
- How will you feel when the change occurs?
- What can you do to reinforce the positive change?
- What will you do as your part in the deal?
- How can you, in turn, meet his needs?

Answering these questions will help you focus on the changes you need in your marriage. You realize that without focus and clarity, you cannot expect any changes in your man.

Change requires, among other things, adhering tenaciously to your plan.

Allowing Consequences

What if you practice all the tools outlined in this book, add a dollop of courage, and still find your man resistant to change? We would be naive if we believed men, and women for that matter, were never resistant to change. After all, who really wants to change, especially if they really don't have to?

Most people do not change until absolutely necessary. We wait until the doctor looks at us square in the eyes and says, "Knee replacement surgery will do no good if you don't lose 40 pounds." *Boom!* Or, "If you don't cut back on your alcohol consumption, your liver will be shot within five years." *Ouch!*

Doctors don't cut us any slack. They have nothing to lose by telling us the truth. But spouses do. So we nag, complain, cajole, harass, scold, and pout. We threaten all kinds of things, then renege and, in essence, say we were just kidding. We often stop short of holding our spouses accountable for change. We drift in and out of complaining. We get depressed, angry, and discouraged, and we wonder why change doesn't occur. (Remember our rule of saying it consistently!)

When you act courageously, you refuse to soften the consequences of your husband's actions. You accept the consequences for your behaviors and afford others the responsibility for their actions. What does this mean to you in your relationship with your husband?

- You thoughtfully consider the logical consequences of his behavior.

- You refuse to continue to coddle him by softening the ground when he falls.

- You care about him, but you don't take care of him.

- You prayerfully consider your part in an issue, take responsibility for it, and separate that responsibility from his part.
- You say things clearly and courageously, which allows him to take responsibility for his actions.

But is this biblical behavior? Yes, it is. Consider with me the teachings of the apostle Paul in Galatians 6.

> Do not be deceived: God cannot be mocked. A man reaps what he sows. The one who sows to please his sinful nature, from that nature will reap destruction; the one who sows to please the Spirit, from the Spirit will reap eternal life. Let us not become weary of doing good, for at the proper time we will reap a harvest if we do not give up (Galatians 6:7-9).

What happens if we interrupt the natural course of sowing and reaping? What if our mate sows seeds of irresponsibility and we interrupt the natural, spiritual course of things? We have seen this happen many times, and the result can be very damaging to us and our mate.

Remember Sandy, hoping beyond hope that she could repair her third marriage but wondering how she could do it? When I discussed these principles with her, she was surprised by my advice. For the first time, someone had actually given her permission to set healthy boundaries in her life. I had dared to voice what she had been thinking for years. She wanted to be firmer with her husband, Kelly. She was ready to talk to him in new ways, absent the whining, complaining, powerless voice she had fallen back on for most of her life.

Sandy is much happier today. She approached Kelly resolutely about reducing their debt and about the importance of making decisions jointly. When he offered initial resistance, she stood her ground. She recognized the importance of his hobbies but also insisted upon being heard regarding her discomfort with large credit card debt. She told Kelly that she did not want to keep working overtime to pay the credit debt down. She was clear, consistent, and courageous. She gilded everything she said with love because she truly wanted to honor Kelly and make their marriage work. Today, they are talking, negotiating a financial plan that works for both of them.

A short time ago, my longtime friend and colleague Tom came into my office. "I need to talk to you," he said soberly.

"What's the matter?" I asked.

"David," he said, "you need to be more available as a leader here at the office. We continue to have staff problems because you are not here enough. You are preoccupied with work and forget to focus on staff morale. We need a leader for organizational issues and staff problems. These problems are not going away, and I'm not going to ignore them any longer. I'm not going to let you ignore them either."

I immediately became defensive. Obviously, I did not want to hear these words and had a ready, reactive response. But I stopped myself before I spoke. I let his words sink in. He had come in to talk to me out of concern. His sentiments were not new. I had heard them before but had hoped the problems would disappear without any adjustment on my part. I had let the periodic complaining go in one ear and out the other. I had dismissed staff morale problems as something every office experiences, something I could do little about. Now, embarrassed, I was faced with the issue again. My friend and colleague was telling me that my actions, or inaction, were causing problems that could no longer be ignored. What would I do?

I decided that the office problems, many of my own making, had to be dealt with. I did not want my staff to feel ignored in any way. I wanted them to feel recognized for the contributions they were making. However, accomplishing this would take work on my part. It would mean going out of my way to notice and acknowledge the positive things my staff was doing. It would mean taking a more active role in solving the organizational problems we faced. It would mean meeting more consistently with the staff to iron out problems so that we could work more effectively as a team. It would take courage to say things that needed to be said, but the results would be worth the effort.

I decided that I would become a more effective leader at the office. I decided to have monthly staff lunches where accomplishments were recognized and we had fun together as a team. I have also lessened my criticisms and taken more time recognizing staff efforts. The results have been very positive.

Avoiding the Power Struggle

As you move into saying things courageously and allowing consequences of actions to play themselves out, you could easily engage in a power struggle. By this, I mean that when you say things clearly, consistently, and courageously, expecting change, your partner may very well say, "Nothing doing! I won't change the way you want me to!" Expect resistance to change. We have difficulty changing our own negative behaviors. We should anticipate similar resistance when we suggest that others need to change. We must remember, however, that this book is not about manipulating your spouse into doing exactly what you want him to do. It is about open, honest, mature communication. And so, on this path toward a more effective expression of your needs, you should expect an occasional slip into the infamous power struggle when stubborn will meets stubborn will.

Michael Gurian, in his book *Love's Journey,* mentions several ways couples shift into power struggles:

- *Direct Control:* Each partner controls a lion's share of the relationship's spiritual process by controlling money or resources, sometimes through physical force.

- *Compliance:* Each partner chooses a strategy of complying with the controller in order to appease. Usually, this compliance finds a compensatory way of controlling, such as passive-aggressiveness.

- *Rebellion:* One or both partners rebel against the relationship's control-based rules and structures.

- *Withdrawal:* One or both partners withdraw emotionally, physically, or financially, through distancing behavior or even divorce.[2]

Perhaps you see yourself in some of the patterns noted above. If so, you are not alone. I often fight the temptation to enter into a power struggle by falling back on passive resistance or withdrawal. At times, I am tempted to appease someone on the outside but resent them inwardly. Entering into a mature relationship where power is shared equally requires work. Only with effort can we resist childish struggles for control.

But if you avoid power struggles, does this guarantee that things will go your way? No. But if you use manipulative tactics to get your way, you are not likely to be happy. No one likes to be manipulated or controlled. Courage is necessary to say things to your mate in a way that allows him to retain his individuality and remain responsible for his own actions.

Rebuilding Courage

Perhaps you have been working at your relationship for a long time and have simply run out of resilience. There is no wellspring of courage left from which to draw.

While tempted to offer platitudes, I will not do so. I too have had seasons in my life when I was so low on courage, so bereft of inner strength, that I could hardly go on. I have felt like the character Tom Hanks plays in *Sleepless in Seattle*. After the tragic loss of his beloved wife, a talk-show host asks him what he's going to do. He replies, "Well, I'm gonna get out of bed every morning...breathe in and out all day long. Then, after a while, I won't have to remind myself to get out of bed every morning and breathe in and out."

We all wonder at times how we can go on. We must remind ourselves that God is our strength, our mighty tower. We must remind ourselves that He employs all our experiences for good, even those we may have trouble dealing with. This knowledge is helpful, but it does not completely remove our discouragement. What else can we do?

Let yourself feel the discouragement. After all, Christ did. The apostles did. Great Christians throughout history have felt discouraged. Discouragement is natural. In fact, it is normal.

Immerse yourself in Scriptures that offer strength. Read Psalms and other Scriptures designed to restore us. Yes, even as we walk through the valley of the shadow of death, the Lord is with us.

Begin, slowly, to rebuild your courage. We do this by taking one small step at a time. Develop a plan of action that is designed to rebuild courage and strength.

- Talk to a friend about your situation.

- Journal about your struggles.

- Walk every day, perhaps by a river or stream.

- Read inspirational material.

- Set healthy boundaries, such as being around positive people and saying no to unhealthy activities.

As you reflect upon what has created discouragement in your life, you will find answers about how to rebuild your courage. As you practice some of the simple steps above, you will become stronger. The more often you say things with courage, even small, simple things, the more courageous you become.

We are now ready to move into our final chapter of this book, where we will explore the ultimate goal—intimacy with one another and God. We experience true happiness in this life when we form a three-part union that includes our spouse, ourselves, and our God. Let's explore together how this exciting intimacy can take place.

Twelve

Communication: Creating Intimacy

For one human being to love another, that is the
work for which all other work is but preparation.

RAINER MARIA RILKE

❧ ✿ ☙

I walked cautiously into the church office and asked the woman seated at her desk if I could see Pastor Carleton. The secretary was friendly enough—had she not been, I might have left immediately.

"Is he expecting you?" she asked politely.

"Yes," I said uneasily. "I called yesterday. He told me to come by today around three."

"Let me see if he is available."

She knocked softly on Pastor Carleton's door, and I heard her explain that I was waiting to see him.

In a moment, she was back. "Go right in," she said.

I hesitantly walked into his office. It seemed rather cold, filled with rows and rows of books, stacked from floor to ceiling. He sat behind a large desk, cluttered with notes and more books. The room was dark, the air stale. How could Pastor Carleton be comfortable in a room like this? There were no posters on the walls—only a picture of Jesus praying, like the one my parents had at home. The portrait seemed so stiff. Did Jesus ever smile? Did He ever laugh and horse around? Did He ever play practical jokes?

"Hello, David. Sit down. So, tell me, are you enjoying high school?"

"Not really. I'm not sure what I am cut out for, but I know it probably isn't school."

"So, what do you like to do?"

"I have a bunch of friends. We play just about every sport; whatever season it is, we're playing it. And I like to watch shows like *The Man from U.N.C.L.E.* I even write stories for fun."

"Really? Do you prefer baseball, basketball, or football?"

"Doesn't really matter to me. Whatever is in season."

"I know what you mean. Well, tell me why you are here."

There I was, a scruffy-haired, baggy-jeaned teenager sitting in a pastor's office. Although I'd grown up in the church, I had never spent much time with the pastor. In fact, I hadn't spent *any* time with the pastor that I could recall, except the occasional small talk over lunch at my parents' home. Now I was second-guessing myself about why I was here.

I had a lot of questions about religion in general and Christianity in particular. I had been taught the basics of the Christian faith, but now, as a 17-year-old, everything seemed confusing. I was no longer sure of what I believed and was even less sure of how to get the answers.

Not only was I confused about my faith, but many other questions also swirled in my mind. If not college, then what? Should I follow my dad in his career as a businessman? Should I join the Army, as my friends had, and risk going to Vietnam? Pastor Carleton seemed the right place to sort things out.

Pastor Carleton was an interesting man. He too seemed to be a misfit. He had longer hair, a full beard, and dressed casually much of the time. For a conservative church, he was a stretch. I often heard murmurings about whether or not he would last in a traditional setting. My parents embraced him because of his warm and loving nature, but they made no bones about the khakis and beard. Not appropriate for a pastor, they would say.

Perhaps that is why he seemed the logical choice for me to share some thoughts and feelings with—information that was too threatening to share with my parents.

I approached Pastor Carleton with a combination of arrogance and confusion. I immediately challenged him on fundamentals of the faith: I wanted to know if he really believed in the things he shared from the pulpit. I went down a laundry list of frustrations I had with Christianity:

- Did he really believe in prayer?
- Could I really expect to pray to Someone, Something, that I couldn't see, and expect to be heard?
- If I was heard, could I expect to be answered?
- And what about this three-in-one God? How was that possible?
- Did Christ really die? If so, how could He possibly rise again?
- If He did rise again, why did He die in the first place?
- Did God have a specific plan for my life? If so, what was it?

I knew the standard answers, but I wanted in-depth explanations about how it all really worked. I was, in essence, asking him if he really truly believed everything he'd learned in seminary. Everything he taught us on Sunday mornings. I never considered that I might be stepping on sacred turf. I never wondered if he would throw me out on my ear for asking such preposterous questions. I had questions, and who was better qualified to answer them than a pastor?

Pastor Carleton was gracious enough to meet with me that day and for many days that followed. He would set his concordances aside, next to his lexicons, and give me his full attention.

He let me talk and think out loud, ultimately arriving at answers to my own questions. He didn't just indulge my questions—I think he enjoyed them. I learned that he was also meeting with college students at our city's university and relished the friendly debate and discussion of issues of faith.

My pastor offered no pie-in-the-sky answers to my questions. No clichés or pat answers that would have reduced the Christian faith to a recipe. After all, if the faith was complex enough to challenge great thinkers like the apostle Paul, I was in good company. If great patriarchs of the faith went through times of weakness and doubt, I did not need to feel so bad as a high schooler for daring to challenge a pastor. If God was truly relevant, He would understand and abide my questions.

Pastor Carleton did not fully satisfy my search for answers, but he did create a safe place for me to explore all my questions. He allowed a relationship to unfold between us—an unlikely friendship, based upon open, honest communication. He did not shame or scold me for asking questions, as I thought some pastors might. He did not intimidate me with spiritual babble. He gave me a safe place to think my thoughts out loud. He created a sanctuary for me. He considered the questions with me.

Like me as a 17-year-old, you will need to find a safe place to ask and answer the deeper questions in your life. I hope that you will press in and seek safety in your marriage. I hope that you will clearly tell your man that you must have safety before you can have other wonderful qualities, such as intimacy, in your marriage.

Safety means that you can say what you need to say, think what you think, and know what you know. All without judgment. I hope, as you practice the tools in this book, you will find your man interested in hearing more of what you have to say.

Our Goal of Intimacy

My pastor and I enjoyed a wonderful give-and-take of ideas. I was able to challenge him without undue defensiveness on his part. He was able to gently point out contradictions in my thinking, which helped me look at myself and my beliefs more closely. I avoided universalizing (saying things like *always* and *never*), which helped the flow of communication. I owned my thoughts and he owned his. Our boundaries were clear. In short, I had safety and an opportunity to think and to be who I was.

If you have been able to create safety in your marriage, you are well on your way to creating intimacy. If you have moved toward intimacy, you already know many skills that aid in this movement. You already know about the importance of owning your thoughts and not telling your partner what he is thinking or what he said. But if you have not been able to create safety, doing so will be one of the primary tasks on the path to true intimacy—the main goal of communication.

You may come to this last chapter with lingering questions. Will these steps really work to help my man listen to me? Can I change my patterns of communication to enhance the possibility that he will truly tune in? What if, after all of this, he chooses not to listen to me?

These are all legitimate questions that beg for answers. Some will be easy to address, some not so easy. Relationships, with your man and with God, cannot be boiled down to one-line responses.

Our objective is complex. Our task is great. Let's remind ourselves of our goals:

- to know what you need in a relationship
- to speak so that he will listen
- to learn new tools to enhance the possibility that he will listen
- to rid ourselves of outdated tools that don't work

- to explore the meaning and purpose of intimacy
- to include God as partner and sustainer in your intimacy

What exactly is intimacy? How does speaking so that he will listen help us to find it? What is God's role in this process? Those are questions we hope to answer in this final chapter.

Many people are confused about the definition of *intimacy*, and clarification is necessary. As we proceed through this chapter, I want to share three intertwined aspects of intimacy. The first is intimacy with self—a vital foundation for intimacy with others. The second is intimacy with your mate. The third is intimacy with God. All parts are necessary if you are to have a balanced and healthy life.

Intimacy with Self

Before we can achieve intimacy with others, we first must have a proper relationship with ourselves. This is a critical concept that we must all understand. In many circles, this language—developing a relationship with ourselves—is considered to be New Age lingo and is summarily dismissed. But brushing it off that easily is a mistake. Those without a healthy sense of self, including a set of effective boundary-setting abilities, are destined to end up in emotional and relational trouble.

Patti was a 38-year-old mother of three when she came for counseling. She had been married for 18 years and was becoming increasingly discouraged about her life and her relationship. She had learned the hard way that if she did not care for herself, she would have little left to care for others.

Her problems began shortly after her marriage to Rick. She didn't know at the time that he struggled chronically with low self-esteem that stemmed from a troubled childhood. He had a pattern of always feeling that the world was out to hamper any progress he tried to make in life. He came home nearly every evening from his job in the printing department of a local newspaper feeling that everyone was getting a better deal than he. He talked to Patti for hours about his woes, never seeming to find a way to make his job satisfying or fulfilling. He was bitter at the boss, other workers, and the company.

Patti tried to help Rick feel better about himself. She spent hours listening to him, encouraging him, insisting that a better day was on the horizon. But it never arrived. In fact, Rick lost ground and slipped into a low-grade depression. This only increased the load Patti was trying to carry.

As if caring for Rick were not enough, she also had a twin sister who relied upon her as well. Her sister, who lived only a few blocks away, called Patti several times a day—sometimes just to chat, but often to talk about the struggles with her alcoholic husband. Patti continued to hone her skills as a caretaker with her husband, sister, and her own children.

Patti finally came to counseling because the demands of life were choking out any ability for her to have fun. Her world, as she described it, was always "heavy, demanding, and serious. I don't have any room for me to enjoy life. Everyone wants a piece of me, and there isn't enough to go around. Rick can't help me because he is always tired and depressed. I feel like the incredible shrinking woman. I'm sure I'm not a lot of fun to be around either."

Over the years, Patti had taken on the "good mother" complex—always doing for others before she did anything for herself. Like many other women, she felt responsible for everyone's moods, for their well-being, for their lives. She lived under the false perception that the world could not function if she didn't help it along.

As we look at Patti's life, we can see that she has distorted her role. She has given up herself in order to please others, something I talk about at length in my book *When Pleasing Others Is Hurting You*. She doesn't realize that to love and be intimate with others requires that she care for herself.

Brennan Manning, in his marvelous book *The Ragamuffin Gospel*, cites Carl Jung, the famous psychiatrist, in discussing a famous Scripture that says, "Whatever you did for the least of these brothers of mine, you did for me." He quotes Jung's probing question: "What if you discovered that the least of the brethren of Jesus, the one who needs your love the most, the one you can help the most by loving, the one to whom your love will be most meaningful—what if you discovered that this least of the brethren of Jesus—is *you?*"[1]

Thomas Merton, the great theologian and philosopher, said something quite similar. He said that the greatest violence we commit in this world is to work ourselves to death. He knew about our anxious strivings and the deleterious effect they have on us.

Slowly, Patti and I worked on setting healthy boundaries. She rediscovered a meaningful relationship with herself by exploring the kinds of activities that gave her joy, such as reading, finding antiques, and hiking.

We determined her responsibilities and the responsibilities of her husband, sister, and children. Patti learned how to share her feelings and needs clearly and consistently to her husband and children. She gave herself permission to be appropriately "selfish." She learned how to set limits on the demands of her sister. Gradually, things began to improve.

Intimacy with Your Mate

I have always taught that intimacy means "into me see." When we are intimate, we allow others to see into us, and we see into them.

I had, in a rough use of the term, achieved intimacy with my former pastor. He created a safe place where I could be vulnerable and ask questions that, to him, may have sounded absurd. But he did not ridicule me. In fact, he honored me for bringing my full self to the relationship. I let down my barriers and allowed him to see me as I was.

I have enjoyed other intimate relationships where I could be myself and be vulnerable. Perhaps you have been fortunate enough to have had similar experiences. Perhaps this book now finds you longing for more of that "safe to be vulnerable" feeling.

Susan Heitler and Abigail Hirsch, in their book *The Power of Two*, share some of their insights about intimacy.

> The term *intimacy* is derived from the Latin word *intimus*, which means innermost. *Innermost* itself is an interesting word, as it means the superlative, or strongest form of, *interior*. That is, intimacy involves sharing the most interior parts of yourself—your most personal and private thoughts, emotions, and physical parts. Intimacy involves an intertwining of the most internally primary parts of your life—how and when and where you eat, sleep, pray, conceive and raise your children, plan for your future and more....
>
> Time refers to how much time you devote to sharing together, and to how long you have known each other. Length of association gives you a sense of "knowing" each other in the sense of familiarity with each other's habits, facial expressions, preferences, values, and other attributes. In successful marriages, those in which communication flows comfortably, the sense of intimate connection, of your lives being deeply intertwined and of knowing each other sexually and emotionally, grows over time.[2]

As Patti's relationship with herself improved and she became clearer about what her responsibilities were and were not, her relationship with her husband also began to improve. Her growth included being more honest with Rick. She shared with him her need to set healthier boundaries. She told him how she felt, trying to be his sole confidant, and she strongly encouraged him to seek professional counsel, which he did. Seeking his own counseling turned out to be a very positive step and led to them participating in couples' counseling as well. At this time their marriage is stronger than ever.

Intimacy with God

No discussion of intimacy is complete without considering our relationship with God. The issue is not whether we *should* talk about our relationship with God. Rather, for the majority of us, when we reflect upon life and how it is going for us, thoughts inevitably turn toward the eternal. In a nutshell, we *must* talk about intimacy with God.

Brennan Manning writes about the "second journey" in our spiritual lives.

> The second journey begins when we know we cannot live the afternoon of life according to the morning program....For the Christian, this second journey usually occurs between the ages of thirty and sixty and is often accompanied by a second call from the Lord Jesus. The second call invites us to serious reflection on the nature and quality of our faith in the gospel of grace, our hope in the new and not yet, and our love for God and people. The second call is a summons to a deeper, more mature commitment of faith where the naivete, first fervor, and untested idealism of the morning and the first commitment have been seasoned with pain, rejection, failure, loneliness, and self-knowledge.[3]

Serious writers who examine the Christian faith often discuss an important truth: God is always calling us, often in new ways according to our life experiences. He wants to have a relationship with us that is honest, candid, and real.

A Pharisee who was an expert on the law asked Jesus what was the greatest commandment in the law.

"'Love the Lord your God with all your heart and with all your soul and with all your mind.' This is the first and greatest commandment. And the second is like it: 'Love your neighbor as yourself'" (Matthew 22:37-39).

God created us for a love relationship with Him. He desperately wants a relationship with us and will pursue us endlessly to have it. I have mentioned this level of intimacy after addressing intimacy with self and mate, but it is actually the foundation for any prosperous relationship. Listen to the words of Moses:

> This day I call heaven and earth as witnesses against you that I have set before you life and death, blessings and curses. Now choose life, so that you and your children may live and that you may love the LORD your God, listen to his voice, and hold fast to him (Deuteronomy 30:19-20).

Henry Blackaby and Claude King, in their book *Experiencing God,* state, "God always takes the initiative in this love relationship. God must take the initiative and come to us if we are to experience Him. This is the witness of the entire Bible."[4] The Lord sought Adam and Eve in the Garden, Saul on the road to Damascus, and the disciples as they cast their nets into the Sea of Galilee. He seeks us out in the particulars of our daily lives and longs to have an intimate relationship with us. Out of that intimacy, He promises to bless us.

The Language of Love

I have tried to create a recipe for successful communication with your man, but that alone is still not enough. Saying things in just the right way is not guaranteed to reach him. Gary Smalley and John Trent write in their book *The Language of Love* that serious problems are created by a "failure to communicate in a meaningful way."[5] A relationship is hardly ever ruined by lack of communication, but more often by an overuse of everyday words that fail to provide insight, intimacy, and understanding.

This was certainly true in Patti's life. Smalley and Trent believe that speaking to your mate in emotional word pictures can be a powerful tool to unlock the hearts of defensive men.

> Unlike anything else we've seen, this concept has the capacity to capture a person's attention by simultaneously engaging a person's thoughts and feelings. And along with its ability to move us to deeper levels of intimacy, it has the staying power to make a lasting impression of what we say and write. With fewer words, we can clarify and intensify what we want to communicate. In addition, it enables us to open the door to needed changes in a relationship.[6]

What exactly is an emotional word picture? It uses a story to simultaneously activate the emotions and intellect. Using this image causes the person to experience your words, not just hear them.

Patti began to illustrate to her husband just how worn out she really was:

- "I feel like I'm caught in a vise. I can't move one way or the other without someone making a demand on my time."

- "I feel like our communication is dry as toast. I want to talk about something moist and wonderful."

- "I feel tired a lot of the time, like I'm walking around with combat boots on."

- "When I'm angry with you it is so hard to be attentive. The anger creates a huge wall between us. I can hardly see you, let alone hear you."

Patti noticed that the more she used these kinds of emotional word pictures, the more Rick seemed to pay attention to her and her needs. This set in motion a positive cycle because she in turn was more willing to listen to his problems and concerns. She found her attitude toward him improving.

We find these kinds of images peppered throughout the Scriptures. Christ, in His parables, almost always used word pictures to illustrate a point. One concerned loving our enemies. In a radical teaching, Christ challenges us to love those that might persecute us. "If you love those who love you, what reward will you get? Are not even the tax collectors doing that? And if you greet only your brothers, what are you doing more than others? (Matthew 5:46-47). The Scriptures challenge us to listen to those with whom we are angry. They challenge us to listen to them in new ways so that we begin to hear what lies beneath their defenses and pain.

Here Christ offers us a picture. *Be like this—not like that. If you do this, you will be like these people, but if you do that, you will be sons of your Father in heaven.*

The language of love asks us to communicate in new ways. It asks us to take all of the tools we have acquired thus far in this book and add emotional word pictures to them for a powerful effect.

The Walls of My Heart

For some, this book finds you in a lonely place, behind thick walls of hurt. Your heart has been broken many times, and you read these words from behind a protective layer you have constructed. I understand. My heart has been broken too, and I have wondered about the wisdom of trusting my feelings to another person again. But something within all of us says, "Try again. You must risk trying again."

I must be clear with you. I am not advocating that you simply place your trust in someone without using wisdom. I do not want you to trust someone who may not be trustworthy. I am not suggesting that you unveil your heart to someone known to be violent or blatantly hurtful. This would be foolish and would run counter to the counsel I have given regarding the laws of sowing and reaping. Distance may be the only practical step when facing someone known to be abusive.

Having said that, no one is perfect. Perfection belongs to God alone. Only you will know when you must take a step back from someone because he or she has caused you too much pain. But I can guarantee that following the counsel in this book will offer you powerful tools for effective communication and ultimate intimacy. Because there may be ways to reach your man, I encourage you to try again, using the tools I have provided. Open your heart to the possibilities that God can perform in your life.

As you try again, take one step at a time. Practice one tool, notice its effect, and then add another. Watch and see how the tools can be used in combination to construct a powerful strategy. Each tool fits together with the others, constructing a place where he will likely to listen and respond. Take the chance.

The Wisdom of My Mother

"Communication is the key," she said softly. "You have to be bold enough to say it the way it is and kind enough to say it with grace."

She smiled at me, and then turned her head slightly and winked at my father. My mother can still melt my heart with her smile. And after 55 years, she is still in love with my father. They are the cutest couple I know, sitting cozily on their couch or toddling along the sidewalk, hand in hand.

I have asked for her wisdom about relating, a subject she seems to know quite intimately. I wanted a few words from her to close this book.

"I am glad that it gets better and better," she said. "Love is far more than a flash in the pan. Anyone can be in love for an hour or a week. The movies make a farce of love. Real love lasts a life-time. It takes dedication and lots of work. Your father has not always been easy to love—but that's not the point. I haven't al-ways been easy to love either. But we're committed to keeping our marriage strong. We are quick to share what is on our minds, quick to listen to each other, and quick to forgive when we have hurt the other's feelings. This recipe seems to work for us."

As she shares these words from her heart, my father sits qui-etly, stroking her hands, affirming her words. He adds a thought here and there, but mostly he is content to let her talk. He puts his arm around her and smiles.

I have watched them closely for the past 20 years. Since about the age of 30 I have been very interested in what they have to say and how they treat each other. And because they seem to know a lot about love and relationships, I listen closely.

More than listening to what they say, I watch what they do. They seem to have a balance in life that illustrates many of the principles I have shared in this book. My parents still enjoy sep-arate activities that feed and renew their spirits. My mother still enjoys her quilting while my father continues to lead singing at the retirement community where they live.

They still enjoy community by attending the same church they helped found 50 years ago. They are, as you might expect, held in high esteem because of their years of devoted service.

The church has afforded them friendships that span more than half a century. They speak fondly of Dwight and Jeanette, Elwood and Erma, and Roy and Gladys. These are names I have heard my entire life. These are couples who played an in-strumental role in my development and are still my parents' friends to this day. My parents have fostered and nurtured these friendships through good times and bad, through times of loss and times of celebration.

More than a place for friends, the church is a place where my parents maintain a peaceful relationship with God. Theirs is a quiet faith. A simple prayer here, a verse of encouragement there. A picture of Christ on the wall as a quiet guest in their home. Strands of a cord woven together to create a strong bond.

And they talk. They communicate with one another—calmly, clearly, and with conviction. Sometimes more firmly than others, but always graciously. Always with the purpose of coming closer together.

And so, as I close the final chapter of this book, I offer my parents' lives as an example of how a relationship can come together for each of us. You can celebrate intimacy with yourself, your mate, and your Lord. This is what life is about.

I wish you peace and strength as you continue your journey in communicating effectively so that you can know intimacy in new and exciting ways.

Notes

Chapter 1—Everybody's Talking At Me

1. Susan Heitler and Abigail Hirsch, *The Power of Two* (Oakland: New Harbinger Publications, 2003), 3.
2. Quoted in Sam Keen, *To Love and Be Loved* (New York: Bantam Books, 1997), 5.
3. Willard Harley Jr., *Love Busters* (Grand Rapids: Baker Book House, 1992), 89.
4. Deborah Tannen, *You Just Don't Understand* (New York: Ballantine Books, 1990), 24.
5. Rosamund Stone Zander and Benjamin Zander, *The Art of Possibility* (Boston: Harvard Business School Press, 2000), 97.
6. Erich Fromm, *The Art of Loving* (New York: Harper & Row, 1956).
7. Daphne Rose Kingma, *The Men We Never Knew* (Emeryville, CA: Conari Press, 1994), 193.

Chapter 2—What's He Hearing?

1. Cranor Graves, *Building a Marriage* (New York: Hyperion, 1993), 14.
2. Ibid., 20.
3. Ruth Painter Randall, *Mary Lincoln* (Boston: Little, Brown and Company, 1953), 18.
4. Ibid., 28.

5. David Clarke, *Men Are Clams, Women Are Crowbars* (Ulrichsville, OH: Barbour Publishing, 1998), 14.

6. Ibid., 65.

Chapter 3—Getting His Attention

1. Sam Keen, *To Love and Be Loved* (New York: Bantam Books, 1997), 40.

2. Ibid.

3. Ibid., 43.

4. Rick Warren, *The Purpose-Driven Life* (Grand Rapids: Zondervan, 2002), 17, 24.

5. Joyce Meyer, *Help Me, I'm Married!* (Tulsa: Harrison House, 2000), 158.

6. David Clarke, *A Marriage After God's Own Heart* (Sisters, OR: Multnomah Publishers, 2001), 38.

Chapter 4—Saying It Calmly

1. John Townsend and Henry Cloud, *Boundaries Face to Face* (Grand Rapids: Zondervan, 2003), 172.

2. Ibid., 173.

3. John Gottman, *The Seven Principles for Making Your Marriage Work* (New York: Three Rivers Press, 1999), 245.

4. Harper Lee, *To Kill a Mockingbird* (Philadelphia: J.B. Lippincott, 1960), 36.

5. Townsend and Cloud, 175-84.

6. Gottman, 6.

7. Ibid., 27-34.

Chapter 5—Saying It Clearly

1. Dorothy Herman, *Helen Keller* (New York: Alfred Knopf, 1998), 12.

2. Ibid., 122.

3. Byron Katie, *Loving What Is* (New York: Harmony Books, 2002), 66.

Chapter 6—Saying It Concisely

1. David Clarke, *Men Are Clams, Women Are Crowbars* (Ulrichsville, OH: Barbour Publishing, 1998), 76.

2. Willard Harley Jr., *Love Busters* (Grand Rapids: Baker Book House, 1992), 85.

Chapter 7—Saying It Compassionately

1. Susan Jeffers, *Opening Our Hearts to Men* (New York: Fawcett Columbine, 1989), 131.

2. Ibid., 134.

3. Paul Tournier, *To Understand Each Other* (Richmond, VA: John Knox Press, 1970), 56.

Chapter 8—Saying It Consistently

1. Virginia Satir, *Making Contact* (Millbrae, CA: Celestial Arts, 1976), 12.
2. David Whyte, *The Heart Aroused* (New York: Doubleday Books, 1994), 175.
3. Laurie Beth Jones, *The Path* (New York: Hyperion, 1996), x.
4. Ibid., xi.
5. Ibid., xvii.

Chapter 9—Saying It with Conviction

1. Ruth Viorst, *Alexander, Who's Not (Do You Hear Me? I Mean It!) Going to Move* (New York: Aladdin Books, 1995), 6.
2. Quoted in Louis Fischer, *The Life of Mahatma Gandhi* (New York: Harper and Row, 1950), 10.

Chapter 10—Saying It with Conciliation

1. Available online at www.ketchum.org/tacomacollapse.html. Accessed July 20, 2004.
2. Quoted in Harville Hendrix, *Getting the Love You Want* (New York: HarperCollins Publishers, 1988), 49.
3. Daphne Rose Kingma, *The Book of Love* (Berkeley: Conari Press, 2001), 152.

Chapter 11—Saying It with Courage

1. David Whyte, *Crossing the Unknown Sea* (New York: Riverhead Books, 2001), 14.
2. Michael Gurian, *Love's Journey* (Boston: Shambhala, 1995), 78.

Chapter 12—Communication: Creating Intimacy

1. Quoted in Brennan Manning, *The Ragamuffin Gospel* (Sisters, OR: Multnomah Publishers, 1990), 174.
2. Susan Heitler and Abigail Hirsch, *The Power of Two* (Oakland, CA: New Harbinger Publications, 2003), 186.
3. Manning, 186.
4. Henry Blackaby and Claude King, *Experiencing God* (Nashville: Broadman and Holman Publishers, 1998), 84.
5. Gary Smalley and John Trent, *The Language of Love* (Colorado Springs: Focus on the Family Publications, 1988), 8.
6. Ibid., 9.

Also by David Hawkins...

When Pleasing Others Is Hurting You

As a servant of Christ, when you begin to forfeit your own God-given calling and identity in an unhealthy desire to please others, you move from servanthood to codependency. This helpful guide can get you back on track.

Does Your Man Have the Blues?

Dr. Hawkins exposes the problem of male depression with unusual compassion and clarity. He describes the telltale signs, pinpoints some of the causes, and suggestys ways you can help your man.

Dr. Hawkins is interested in hearing about your journey and may be contacted through his website at InCourageMinistry.com

HARVEST HOUSE
PUBLISHERS

Title Withdrawn